THE JOHNS HOPKINS UNIVERSITY STUDIES IN HISTORICAL AND POLITICAL SCIENCE

Under the Direction of the Departments of History,
Political Economy, and Political Science

SERIES LXVIII   NUMBER 2
(1950)

Johns Hopkins University
Studies in historical and political science

THE THEORY OF INTER-SECTORAL MONEY FLOWS AND INCOME FORMATION

BY

JOHN SOMERSET CHIPMAN

BALTIMORE
THE JOHNS HOPKINS PRESS
1951

PRINTED IN THE UNITED STATES OF AMERICA
BY J. H. FURST CO., BALTIMORE, MARYLAND

TO MY FATHER

CONTENTS

7

PREFACE

The Development of the Work

This work began as part of a Master of Arts thesis at McGill University under the direction of Professor Donald B. Marsh, and was completed as a dissertation for the degree of Doctor of Philosophy at The Johns Hopkins University under Professor Fritz Machlup.

Much of the present study has already appeared in published form. Chapter 4 was published (with slight difference in terminology) under the title " The Generalized Bi-System Multiplier," in the *Canadian Journal of Economics and Political Science,* Vol. XV, No. 2 (May, 1949). This article was drawn from Part II of my Master's thesis, and reorganized along lines suggested by Professor G. A. Elliott, Managing Editor of the *Canadian Journal.*

Material contained in Section IV of Chapter 3, Chapter 6, Sections I to III of Chapter 7, and Section I of Chapter 8, appeared under the title "The Multi-Sector Multiplier," in *Econometrica,* Vol. 18, No. 4 (October, 1950). This paper was originally presented under the title "The Multi-Part Multiplier" in a session on the "Analysis of the Multi-Part Economy" at the New York Meeting of the Econometric Society, December 28, 1949. It was later revised on the basis of constructive suggestions made by the editors of *Econometrica.*

Finally, a considerable amount of material appeared in an article entitled "Professor Goodwin's Matrix Multiplier," in the *Economic Journal,* Vol. LX, No. 240 (December, 1950); this is contained in Section IV of Chapter 2, Sections II and III of Chapter 3, Chapter 6, and Sections III and IV of Chapter 7. This article is a criticism and development of ideas put forward by Professor R. M. Goodwin in his paper "A Matrix Multiplier," presented at the same session of the Econometric Society as my paper "The Multi-Part Multiplier," and published in the *Economic Journal* under the title " The Multiplier as Matrix."

The material taken from the above journals is reproduced with the kind permission of the editors.

The Use of Terminology

In attempting to adapt existing theoretical formulations to new uses, considerable difficulty in terminology was experienced. The retention of the Keynesian expression "marginal propensity" (already a strain on language in Keynes' *General Theory*) led inevitably to awkward terms such as the "marginal propensity to pay taxes" and "marginal propensity to export"; the Keynesian terminology is so universally accepted, however, that it would only add to the confusion if another expression were invented for the conception which it denotes.

The application of a theoretical framework previously designed for the analysis of international trade, to other provinces of economics—such as interregional trade, the theory of distribution, and the analysis of interindustrial relationships—necessitated some changes in terminology. Thus "foreign balance" became "external balance," and "countries" became "sectors."

On the whole, the terminology used in my work has undergone considerable change since this study was first begun. In my *Canadian Journal* article I spoke of "systems" and of the "multi-system multiplier," following the terminology of Oscar Lange. Professor Machlup objected to this phrase, however, contending that the term "system" referred more properly to a body of thought or to a whole composed of parts than to the parts themselves. I later used the term "multi-part multiplier" at the suggestion of Professor Harold Somers, of the University of Buffalo. At Professor Machlup's persuasion, I finally settled upon the term "sector."

It is difficult, in a study of this sort, to describe precise concepts in language that was devised for other purposes. I hope the reader will be forgiving, therefore, if the style is in places pedantic and clumsy.

The Nature of the Work

The present study is entirely theoretical in nature. There are several reasons for this. In the first place, the development of the theoretical framework is a large enough task in itself to justify independent treatment. Secondly, many useful conclusions may be drawn from the purely theoretical discussion without recourse to extensive empirical research. Finally, much information is as yet unavailable (especially data required for regional studies), so that empirical application of the theory in certain fields is impossible at this time.

The theoretical treatment employs a considerable amount of mathematics. Part I, however, does without mathematics, and Part II employs only elementary algebra and a slight amount of calculus. In Part III, substantial use is made of matrices, difference equations, and complex numbers. Since few economists today are equipped with this mathematical knowledge, I have taken care in Chapter 6 to ease the task of the reader by going through all the necessary steps. The mathematics may therefore be intelligible to the reader who has but an elementary knowledge of matrices and of trigonometrical functions.

I have found from experience that in a subject as complex as the present one, it is very easy to draw erroneous conclusions from intuition, verbal reasoning, and numerical examples. In making generalizations I have therefore relied as much as possible upon mathematical proof. To those who may suggest that some of my conclusions are too obvious to require mathematical proof, I can only reply that they were not obvious to me, and that some propositions which I thought to be obvious turned out later to be true only under certain circumstances which do not necessarily hold in the real world.

Acknowledgments

The research for this book was made possible by the awards, first, of a Special Scholarship in Political Economy and, later, of the Gustav Bissing Fellowship, at The Johns Hopkins University. Financial assistance was also received from the Lessing Rosenthal Fund for Economic Research at The Johns Hopkins University. Grateful acknowledgment is due to Professor G. Heberton Evans, Jr., for his many favors and kindnesses which greatly facilitated my research.

I am greatly indebted to Professor Alfred H. Clifford, of the Department of Mathematics at The Johns Hopkins University, for his invaluable mathematical assistance. Much of the mathematics in section I and III of Chapter 7 is due to him, and section I could not have been written without his help. I provided the theorems and he furnished the proofs. I have also had the benefit of mathematical advice from Professor Aurel Wintner and Dr. Ta-Chung Liu, both of The Johns Hopkins University, and Professor Lloyd Metzler, of the University of Chicago.

I have much benefited from stimulating discussions with Professor Donald B. Marsh, and have greatly profited from the advice of Professor Clarence D. Long, who read the manuscript and offered many valuable criticisms and suggestions. Much valuable advice, particularly with regard to presentation, was received from Mr. Stanley B. Kurta.

I was fortunate in having much thought-provoking discussion and correspondence with Professor R. M. Goodwin, of Harvard University. While I found several objections to Goodwin's paper on the matrix multiplier, which was developed completely independently of my formulation, his different approach was the source of much stimulation, and did much to clarify the multiplier process in my own mind. I also benefited from discussing many questions with Professor Paul A. Samuelson, of the Massachusetts Institute of Technology.

Acknowledgment must also be made to Mr. E. O. Edwards, Professor G. A. Elliott, Professor Werner Hochwald, Professor Everett E. Hagen, Professor Evsey D. Domar, Professor Arnold C. Harberger, and Mr. Joel Levy.

Above all, I am indebted to Professor Fritz Machlup. It was his work that first stimulated my interest in the theory of the multiplier, and assured my continued interest in economic theory. It was indeed fortunate for me to complete this study under his direction. His careful scrutiny of the manuscript, his painstaking page-by-page criticism of the subject-matter and style, and his patient efforts to persuade me to make the analysis clearer and more intelligible, have all been of immense value.

Any errors, defects, or awkwardness of style are, of course, my own responsibility.

J. S. C.

CHAPTER 1

INTRODUCTION

Aggregative economic analysis, as developed by Lord Keynes and his followers, represents a major advance in economic theory. There are, however, certain inherent weaknesses involved in the process of aggregation which make Keynesian economics an unsatisfactory tool in the analysis of income flows. Direct empirical application of Keynesian theory has shown that it is not an adequate tool of analysis for forecasting purposes. This is due in great measure to the fact that the Keynesian aggregates are agglomerations of heterogeneous quantities rather than reasonably homogeneous variables; they need to be decomposed into their constituent parts. It is the purpose of this work to partly overcome this limitation in Keynesian economics by using the tool of matrix algebra to analyze the economy divided into its component economic groups and organisms.

Fundamental to the Keynesian theory is the assumption of a stable relationship between aggregate production of consumer's goods, and aggregate income (the so-called " consumption function "). This function is, as we shall show, derived in a certain way from the functional relationships, pertaining to all economic organisms, between their disbursements and their receipts. Instability in the aggregate functional relationship may result from instability in the individual ones; it may also result, however, from the mere process of aggregation itself.

In addition to aggregating the functional relationships between the disbursements and receipts of different economic organisms, in order to obtain the consumption function, aggregative economics, as developed dynamically, usually deals with a single uniform time lag between changes in income and changes in the production of consumers' goods. The unrealistic nature of this assumption seriously hampers the effectiveness of aggregative dynamic economics.

Our aim is to borrow from international trade theory the

concept of the "foreign trade multiplier" and to apply it to significant economic groups and organisms within an economic system; these groups may include individuals and households, single firms and whole industries, or they may be classes, regions, and governments.

The theory of the multiplier, as first developed by Mr. R. F. Kahn [1] and Lord Keynes,[2] related the change in aggregate income brought about by an initial change in expenditure (such as investment or public expenditure) to the amount of the initial change in expenditure. This multiplier was applicable only to closed economy. Later writers, beginning with Mr. R. F. Harrod,[3] redefined the multiplier concept in order to take account of the leakages of income flows into imports as well as the leakages into savings. This refinement did not, however, take account of what Professor Fritz Machlup was later to call "foreign repercussions"; that is, it did not take account of the fact that the leakages out of the home country's income into imports affected other countries' incomes and imports, and hence affected their spending in the home country.

With the taking into account of the repercussions on a country's income of its spending in another country, the theory of the multiplier took a completely new and significant turn. This development was achieved independently by several writers. The most comprehensive treatment of the subject was Professor Machlup's work, *International Trade and the National Income Multiplier.*[4] Previous to the publication of this work there appeared an article by Professor Lloyd Metzler, "Underemployment Equilibrium in International Trade,"[5] in which were derived the basic formulas for the multiplier in a two-country economy, and the conditions for the stability of such an economy. Subsequently there appeared an article by

---

[1] "The Relation of Home Investment to Unemployment," *Economic Journal,* XLI (June, 1931), 173-198.

[2] *The General Theory of Employment. Interest and Money* (London, 1947).

[3] For a discussion of the formulations of Mr. Harrod and others, see Gottfried Haberler, *Prosperity and Depression* (3d ed., New York, United Nations, 1946, Part III). See also the interesting formulation in R. F. Bretherton, F. A. Burchardt and R. S. G. Rutherford, *Public Investment and the Trade Cycle* (Oxford, England, 1941), pp. 332-336.

[4] Philadelphia, 1943.

[5] *Econometrica,* Vol. 10, No. 2 (April, 1942), pp. 97-112.

Professor Oscar Lange, "The Theory of the Multiplier,"[6] in which a similar formulation was presented. These three formulations of the multiplier for a two-country economy are equivalent; they are shown in Part II of this book to be all special cases of a more general formulation.

Dr. Lange's article contained a significant suggestion, namely, that the two-country multiplier could be applied not only to countries but also to any "systems" such as, for instance, the Treasury and the private economy, and the socialized and nonsocialized sectors of a mixed economy. In pursuing this suggestion, it occurred to me that the economy could also be divided into classes (such as workers and capitalists) and geographical areas (such as advanced and backward regions); I was more and more impressed by the fact that the foreign trade multiplier was a powerful tool of analysis which could be applied to an economy divided into a number of significant functional, as well as regional, divisions.[7]

In addition to applying this tool of analysis to sectors other than countries, I undertook to extend it to more than two sectors, the aim being to formulate a model of an economy divided into n sectors. This had already been done by Professor Machlup, but under very limited assumptions with regard to the similarity of different countries' spending patterns. After my investigation had been well under way, I noticed that the basis of this development had already been provided by Professor Paul A. Samuelson in his article, "A Fundamental Multiplier Identity,"[8] in which an n-country model was briefly stated as a sidelight to his main theme. The basic properties of such a model, however, still remained to be established.

In the process of extending the foreign trade multiplier analysis both quantitatively (to comprise more than two sectors) and qualitatively (to comprise sectors other than

[6] *Econometrica,* Vol. 11, Nos. 3 & 4 (July-October, 1943), pp. 227-245.

[7] It has been pointed out to me by Professor Donald B. Marsh that previous economists have made use of foreign trade theory for the analysis of economics divided into various groupings, viz.: C. F. Bastable, *Theory of International Trade* (London, 1903), p. 13; J. E. Cairnes, *Some Leading Principles of Political Economy* (New York, 1874), p. 193; and F. Y. Edgeworth, *Papers Relating to Political Economy* (London, 1925), Vol. II, Section IV.

[8] *Econometrica,* Vol. 11, Nos. 3 & 4 (July-October, 1943).

countries) it became evident to me that my analysis closely resembled that of Professor Wassily Leontief,[9] in which the economy is divided into a large number of industries. Thus, starting on the basis of Keynesian economics as developed by Machlup, Metzler, Lange, and Samuelson, I arrived at a goal reached by Professor Leontief on the basis of Classical economics as developed by Quesnay, Cournot, Walras, and Pareto. After I had reached this goal, Professor R. M. Goodwin's article, " The Multiplier as Matrix," [10] appeared, in which he developed a multiplier along the lines of the Leontief model, and also noticed the remarkable similarity between the two approaches. Later a very similar article by Professor Metzler also appeared.[11]

While the Leontief model may formally be considered as a special case of a more general model, such as that presented in this book, in which the economy may be divided into many categories in addition to industrial ones, the present work differs substantially in character and emphasis from that of Professor Leontief; the two approaches should be considered as complementary rather than competing. We shall be concerned less with technical coefficients of production and planned bills of goods—essential in the Leontief approach—and more with the effects of injections of expenditure throughout the economy on the flow of income through its various sectors.

Our basic model is, conceptually, a very simple one. The economy is divided into n sectors which are chosen on the basis of a number of economic considerations. It is theoretically possible to go so far as to divide the economy into all its economic organisms—its individuals or households, firms and governments. The way in which, and the extent to which, these

[9] The Structure of American Economy, 1919-1929 (Cambridge, Massachusetts, 1941) ; also " Output, Employment, Consumption, and Investment," Quarterly Journal of Economics, Vol. 58, No. 2 (February, 1944), and " Exports, Imports, Domestic Output, and Employment," Quarterly Journal of Economics, Vol. 60, No. 2 (February, 1946). This similarity to Leontief's work was first suggested to me by Dr. Evsey D. Domar.
[10] Economic Journal, LIX (December, 1949).
[11] Lloyd A. Metzler, " A Multiple-Region Theory of Income and Trade," Econometrica, Vol. 18, No. 4 (October, 1950), pp. 329-354. See also his " Stability of Multiple Markets: The Hicks Conditions," ibid., Vol. 13, No. 4 (October, 1945), pp. 277-292.

organisms should be grouped, depends upon a number of factors which we shall discuss, including the particular purpose for which the analysis is being used. We set up, as delineating the basic forces governing this system, two universal postulates: (1) each sector's disbursements to every sector are a given linear function of its receipts; (2) changes in disbursements follow changes in receipts after a specified time lag.

These postulates are, to be sure, an insufficiently realistic description of the actual forces governing the economy. It is possible, however, by means of certain devices, to increase the applicability of the model within the framework of these postulates. In Part I of this book it is shown that certain changes in definitions of receipts and disbursements (such as the treatment of certain receipts as negative disbursements, and certain disbursements as negative receipts) may make the first postulate more applicable. It is also shown that to the extent that the first postulate does not hold, because sectors disburse different kinds of receipts in different ways, it is possible to make it hold by conceptually dividing such sectors into a number of parts. Finally it is shown that the second postulate may be made to hold by a device of introducing the concept of " goblins " or " collecting agencies." These devices, which will be explained in the following chapters, all serve to set up a model which, whilst remaining within the framework of our two postulates, is in the closest possible conformity, allowed by the limitations of that framework, with the forces which govern the real world.

There are additional deviations of the real world from our two postulates which cannot be handled by the devices introduced in Part I. Thus there may be important factors influencing consumer expenditures other than current incomes;[12] and firms' disbursements may be related not only to their receipts but also to the rate of change of their receipts (the " acceleration principle "). In addition, changes in prices and interest rates, as well as factors such as technological innovation and business psychology, have an important place in the real world.

---

[12] These may include such factors as the real value of consumers' assets (cf. A. C. Pigou, " The Classical Stationary State," *Economic Journal*, LIII [December, 1943]), and possibly others (cf. James S. Duesenberry, *Income, Saving, and the Theory of Consumer Behavior* [Cambridge, Mass., 1949]).

Some of these factors may be taken into account by refinements which are suggested in the final chapter; any attempt, however, to take full account of these phenomena in this work would lead us beyond the scope of our present analysis, and must be reserved for later consideration.

The present work consists of three parts. In Part I, the model is described, and the devices mentioned above are introduced in order to increase the applicability of our two postulates. The special assumptions involved in the Classical and Keynesian theories are described in terms of our model.

Part II consists of a generalized formulation of the multiplier for two sectors. In these chapters, it is shown that the formulas developed by Machlup, Metzler, and Lange are equivalent, and are formally all special cases of a more general formulation.

Part III is the development of Part II into a model for a multi-sector economy, and a derivation of the properties of this system; it is this part which is the core of our work.

PART I

THE MODEL

Chapter 2

DISSECTING THE ECONOMY

I. The Multiplier Process

For purposes of analysis, the economy may be divided into n sectors; these sectors may be organisms or groups of organisms. Each of these sectors receives in-payments of money per unit of time (receipts) and disburses out-payments of money per unit of time (disbursements). According to the basic postulates governing this system, every sector's disbursements in all directions are related in a precise way to its previously acquired receipts from various sources. Any change in the rate at which money is being received by a sector will, after a certain lapse of time, bring about a corresponding change in the rate at which money is being disbursed by it in all directions.[1] This relationship between a sector's disbursements to each of the other sectors as well as to all organisms within itself, and its total receipts from all sectors, at a previous time, may be called its disbursement function. The proportion between the change in a sector's disbursements to any sector and the previous change in its total receipts, may be called its marginal propensity to spend to that sector; and the proportion between the change in its total disbursements and the previous change in its total receipts may be called its marginal propensity to spend.

A sector may disburse its receipts to organisms within itself as well as to other sectors, and receive disbursements from organisms within itself as well as from other sectors. The receipts of any organism from other organisms are, of course,

---

[1] It is avowedly unrealistic to assume that an individual will wait for a lapse of time after a change in his receipts before making any alterations in his disbursements, and then, after the period has elapsed, make all the induced alterations in his disbursements at once. In reality the individual will make alterations in his disbursements continuously throughout this time interval. It is quite possible to allow for this continuous reaction by describing the economy by a system of integro-functional equations, rather than by a system of difference equations. The reader is referred to Lange, " The Theory of the Multiplier," pp. 241-244, and Samuelson, " A Fundamental Multiplier Identity," p. 224n.

the same as the disbursements by the other organisms to the organism in question. Since these disbursements are functionally related to the other organisms' receipts, it follows that the receipts of the organism in question are dependent upon the previous receipts of the other organisms. Every organism's receipts are dependent upon the previous receipts of the other $n - 1$ organisms; the economy is in complete dynamic interdependence. Any disturbance in any part of the economy (such as a rise in a sector's rate of disbursements made possible by the spending of newly-created or newly-activated funds) will have repercussions on the entire economy; disbursements will change in accordance with the disbursement functions, and since these disbursements are also receipts, receipts will keep adjusting themselves to new levels, period by period, until a final equilibrium is reached. This is the well-known "multiplier process"; the multiplier for any sector is the ratio of the final [2] change in its receipts to the initial disturbance. If each sector's marginal propensity to spend to every sector is known, it is possible, mathematically, to calculate the value of the multiplier; this will be done in Part III.

II. THE FOUR MAIN DIVISIONS

It is convenient for conceptual purposes, and as a first step, to divide the economy into four broad categories: Households, Business, Finance, and Government. Households are defined to include all "recipients of income," where income is defined in the national income sense.[3] Since retained corporate profits are part of income,[4] they may be regarded as paid out to a

[2] The multiplier may be defined alternatively as the ratio, to the initial disturbance, of the change in a sector's receipts after a specified (rather than infinite) period of time. Cf. Fritz Machlup, "Period Analysis and Multiplier Theory," *Quarterly Journal of Economics,* LIV (November, 1939), reprinted in *Readings in Business Cycle Theory* (Philadelphia, 1944), pp. 219-220. This is what Professor Samuelson has called the "truncated multiplier" ("A Fundamental Multiplier Identity," p. 222).

[3] Alternative national income concepts may be used, such as gross or net national product at market prices, net national income at factor cost, disposable income, or income paid out. For our purposes the most useful concept is that of income paid out plus undistributed profits.

[4] It is quite possible to use a definition of national income which excludes retained profits. In this case the latter may simply be regarded as hoarding.

group called "earners of retained profits." Households then consist of earners of retained profits as well as of individuals who have really collected their incomes. Business is defined as the sector of sellers (other than Households) of goods and services, and Finance as the sector of sellers of obligations or evidences of debt. Government includes national, regional, and municipal governments.

In actuality, these groups are not completely distinct. Financial establishments perform services essential to their financial functions, as evidenced by interest on loans and service charges for cheque accounts, and engage, therefore, in business activity; in addition, they engage to a considerable extent in business activity unessential to their financial functions, such as the leasing of safe deposits. To the extent that they engage in business activity, financial establishments should be considered analytically as part of Business.

Business establishments, likewise, may engage to a certain extent in financial activity, such as the granting of installment loans; in their latter capacity they should be considered part of Finance. Households may engage in both business and financial activities. To the extent that they engage in the latter, they should be regarded as part of Finance; and insofar as they engage in the former it is likewise preferable to regard them as part of Business, except when all their receipts are net income (as in the case of wage and salary earners, recipients of property income, domestic servants, individual landlords, etc.). Farmers, professionals, and other entrepreneurs should be regarded as part of Households to the extent of their entrepreneurial net income; that is to say, that part of their business receipts which is entrepreneurial net income should be considered as paid out to them, as individuals, by their business. Finally, those business activities which are integral parts of government budgets (such as the sale of postal services) shall be regarded as belonging to the Government sphere; others (such as the activities of government-owned enterprises) are best considered as belonging to the Business sphere.[5]

[5] Certain institutions do not fit well into any of our categories; classification of them is arbitrary. Charitable institutions, for instance, may be regarded as " private governments."

Financial Transactions

Payments for evidences of debt behave in a different fashion, from the point of view of disbursement functions, from other kinds of payment.

Non-financial economic organisms base their disbursements on their non-financial receipts; that is, an organism does not decide upon its disbursements on the basis of its borrowings, but, on the contrary, decides upon its borrowings on the basis of its planned disbursements; and these disbursements are planned with reference to its receipts of money other than those which are in return for evidences of debt. For example, if Households have a greater than unit marginal propensity to spend to Business, they may finance the excess by borrowing from Finance; the borrowings must not be included in the income on the basis of which the disbursement function is drawn. Thus, from the point of view of non-financial sectors' disbursement functions, *all* payments for evidences of debt—in-payments as well as out-payments—should be treated as *disbursements*: out-payments (purchases of evidences of debt, or lending, by non-financial sectors) as *positive* disbursements to Finance, and in-payments (sales of evidences of debt, or borrowing, by non-financial sectors) as *negative* disbursements to Finance.

Just as all payments for evidences of debt shall be regarded as disbursements from the point of view of non-financial sectors, they are to be considered as receipts from the point of view of Finance; thus a loan by another sector to Finance is a positive receipt by Finance from that sector, and a loan from Finance to another sector is a negative receipt by Finance from that sector.

Since all payments (made or received) for evidences of debt must be regarded as disbursements (positive or negative) from the point of view of non-financial sectors, it is impossible—within our conceptual framework—for evidences of debt to be bought and sold among non-financial sectors; for what is a disbursement (positive or negative) from the point of view of the payer is a receipt (positive or negative) from the point of view of the payee. Thus the purchase by Households of private securities cannot be regarded as a disbursement to

Business, for then it would be part of Business' receipts on the basis of which it is supposed to plan its disbursements; the purchase of new private securities (Households' lending to Business) must instead be considered as a positive disbursement from Households to Finance (which is, of course, a positive receipt by Finance) accompanied by a negative disbursement by Business to Finance (which is, of course, a negative receipt of Finance from• Business). Similarly, the private purchase of government bonds must be regarded as done through the intermediary of Finance; for Government does not determine its expenditures on the basis of its borrowing, but determines them independently or with reference to its tax and other revenues.[6]

The External Balances, Money Creation, and Hoarding

The receipts from Households of the three groups—Business, Finance, and Government—correspond to three kinds of Household disbursements—consumption, savings, and taxes (including payment for government services).[7] Households' receipts from Households and Business are private expenditure (consumption and investment), and Households' receipts from Government are public expenditure. We may consider Households, Business, and Government, as three "countries" in "trade" whose in-payments from and out-payments to each other may be regarded as exports and imports respectively; Households' "external balance"[8] (savings) is equal (with opposite signs) to the sum of Business' external balance (investment[9]) and Government's external balance (the budget deficit).

The payments among the four sectors of the economy are

[6] We therefore avoid the unusual procedure adopted by Dr. Lange who includes securities in the private economy's marginal propensity to pay the Treasury (the "Treasury's *marginal propensity to tax and borrow*") ("The Theory of the Multiplier," p. 234) and foreign securities in a country's marginal propensity to import (*ibid.*, p. 233n).

[7] Part of consumption, nevertheless (Households' disbursements to Households, or "intraspending"), does not go to Business, and part of savings (hoarding) does not go to Finance.

[8] This term is defined as the balance of payments exclusive of payments for evidences of debt, that is, exclusive of net payments to Finance. Thus, it includes gifts.

[9] Some peculiar conditions in which this is not so are discussed in the appendix to this chapter.

tabulated in the adjoining table. The elements in each row are the sources of receipt of the sector named at the left of that row, and the elements in each column represent the distribution of the disbursements of the sector named at the head of that column. These inter-sectoral payments are also sketched diagrammatically in Figure 1.

Since, by defintion, every disbursement is at the same time— from the point of view of the sector to which it is disbursed— a receipt, total receipts must be equal to total disbursements. Total payments in the economy will be greater than the algebraic sum of receipts or disbursements because of the peculiar way in which financial transactions are treated in our model. Three kinds of payments may be distinguished: (1) payments for goods and services (commodity transactions); (2) payments for evidences of debt (financial transactions); and (3) payments for nothing, i. e., transfer payments and taxes (donations).

We may further classify payments in a three-fold division according to the sources and destinations of the funds employed: funds are either (1) actively passing from sector to sector in a circular flow throughout the economy, (2) being withdrawn from or added to idle balances or hoards, or (3) being created or destroyed. In equilibrium there is a constant stream of payments, and the quantity of active money remains the same; the algebraic sum of all activation and inactivation of money and creation and destruction of money must be equal to zero. It is the peculiarity of Finance that it is the only sector which (a) deals exclusively in evidences of debt, and (b) creates and destroys money. This power to create and destroy money is the property of a particular branch of Finance, namely the central and commercial banking system. All creation and destruction of money is carried out by the banking system alone,[10] and all activation and inactivation of money (hoarding and dishoarding) is carried out by non-banking sectors alone. If the banking system's net receipts are positive, it is borrowing or collecting more than it is lending; this excess intake of money is destroyed, since the banking system is assumed not to keep

---

[10] It is out of fashion for governments to print money, and against the law— or at least against the postulates of our model—for any other sectors to do so.

	Households	Business	Finance	Government	Total
Households	Households' payments for non-manufactured commodities	Wages, profits and entrepreneurial net income		Government payments of salaries, transfer payments and interest on debt	Total Receipts of Households
Business	Households' payments for manufactured commodities	Inter-firm transactions		Government payments for manufactured commodities, business subsidies and interest on debt	Total Receipts of Business
Finance	Households' net payments for evidences of debt	Net decrease * in business capital and debt		Net decrease * of government debt	Total Receipts of Finance
Government	Household taxes and payments for government services	Business taxes and payments for government services		Grants-in-aid	Total Receipts of Government
	Total Disbursements of Households	Total Disbursements of Business	Total Disbursements of Finance	Total Disbursements of Government	Total Transactions

* If the items in these boxes are negative (as they are likely to be if investment and government deficit are both positive) their absolute value will represent a net *increase* in business and government debt, respectively.

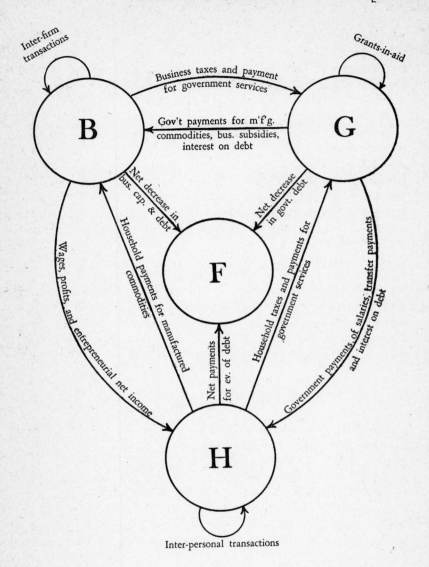

Figure 1.

The circles represent the various sectors, Households, Business, Government, and Finance, which are indicated by their initials. The arrows represent payments of money per unit of time.

"idle balances." Similarly if the banking system's net receipts are negative, it is lending more than it is borrowing or collecting, which it can do only by creating new funds. The net receipts of the banking system are then equal to the increase in the quantity of money if negative, and to the decrease in the quantity of money if positive.

A sector's balance of payments is the excess of its total receipts over its total disbursements. The balance of payments of a sector other than the banking system is hoarding if positive, and dishoarding if negative. The balance of payments of the banking system is the same as its net receipts (since the banking system makes no disbursements, but has positive or negative receipts), and is therefore equal to the fall in the quantity of money if positive, and to the rise in the quantity of money if negative.

In a state of equilibrium, the algebraic sum of all balances of payments must be equal to zero, so that total disbursements are equal to total receipts.[11] Consequently the increase or decrease in the quantity of money is always, in equilibrium, balanced by dishoarding or hoarding; that is, expansion or contraction by the banking system is always offset by contraction or expansion elsewhere in the economy.

III. THE DISBURSEMENT FUNCTIONS OF THE FOUR DIVISIONS

The four divisions of the economy—Households, Business, Finance, and Government—are, of course, not homogeneous groups, and a subdivision of them is desirable.

Households contain classes and cultural groups whose marginal propensities to spend vary considerably. Workers and capitalists will have different marginal propensities to consume, which means that they have different marginal propensities to spend to Business.[12] Individuals in different income-groups will

---

[11] In the *ex post* sense, according to which all payments at a point of time are in "instantaneous equilibrium," the algebraic sum of the balances of payments is always zero, so that receipts and disbursements are always equal, or more accurately, identical.

[12] The marginal propensity to consume and Households' marginal propensity to spend to Business correspond very closely, but not entirely; there will be a

also have different "marginal propensities to pay taxes"[13] to Government, owing to the progressiveness of the tax structure. Furthermore, the artificially defined group of earners of retained profits will have a zero marginal propensity to spend to Business and a unit marginal propensity to spend to Finance.[14] It will therefore be desirable to break down the Households sector into more homogeneous classes—workers, capitalists, earners of retained profits, and others—or into regional groupings, or perhaps, for certain purposes, into many more subdivisions.

The marginal propensities to spend of firms in the Business sector are closely related to their technical coefficients of production. The ratios of changes in a firm's inputs of materials and of services of factors of production, to changes in the firm's output, are its technical coefficients of production. With given prices, the ratios of the values of changes in inputs to the value of changes in output are equivalent to the technical coefficients of production.[15] If there are no changes in inventories or prices, the value of output and the value of sales will also be equivalent. Under these assumptions, therefore, the ratios between changes in the value of inputs to changes in the value of sales will likewise be equivalent to the technical production coefficients.[16] Under certain conditions, therefore,

---

discrepancy between the two to the extent that part of consumption expenditures are interpersonal payments (i. e., between members of the Households sector, chiefly for personal services), and to the extent also that part of the purchases from Business are for capital goods rather than consumption goods.

[13] I am persuaded by Professor Machlup to note that this so-called "propensity" is "shaped by law with sanctions provided for non-conformance."

[14] We shall consider earners of retained profits to save all their receipts, that is, to disburse their receipts to Finance; the process known as the "ploughing back of profits" shall therefore be considered as consisting of three payments: (1) a positive disbursement from Business to Households, (2) a positive disbursement from Households to Finance, and (3) a negative disbursement from Business to Finance. In this way the ploughing back of retained profits is treated as a function of Business receipts, and not as a function of retained profits themselves.

[15] The units in which inputs and outputs are measured may be chosen, without loss of generality, in such a way as to make all prices equal to unity. Values and quantities are then the same, and the above equivalence therefore holds. We may note, further, that it is not necessary in our analysis for production functions to be homogeneous; it is sufficient that they be linear. We do not assume, as Leontief does, that the technical coefficients of production are the same as the firms' *average* propensities to spend.

[16] If certain assumptions are made with regard to perfect complementary or

firms' marginal propensities to spend will be technological in nature. Since these technological aspects of firms' disbursement functions are dealt with in a most thorough manner by Professor Leontief in his study, we shall not attempt to elaborate them here; and since the scope of the present study is of a more broad theoretical nature than his, we shall deal with general disbursement functions that are not necessarily technological, even though the lack of the special Leontief assumptions makes our functional relationships less stable and precisely defined than his.

Owing to the wide degree of diversity among different industries, it is inadvisable to treat Business as a homogeneous group except for the purposes of broad theoretical discussion. Business' marginal propensity to spend will differ according to the particular industries in which any initial disturbance may occur. The extent to which it is desirable to subdivide the Business sector will be discussed in the next chapter.

The financial sector of the economy is composed of the banking system and other financial establishments. Since the disbursements of the non-financial sectors of the economy, as we have seen, are a function of their non-financial receipts, and not of their financial receipts, we choose to regard all payments from Finance to non-financial sectors for evidences of debt as the latter's negative disbursements to Finance. Analogously, Finance is regarded in our model as making no disbursements, but rather as having positive and negative receipts; and changes in its net receipts as regarded as determined by changes in the net disbursements to Finance by the other sectors. Finance's marginal propensity to spend is therefore taken as zero.

In reality, however, changes in Finance's net receipts may bring about changes in the rate of interest, which in turn may bring about further changes in Finance's net receipts by means of changing other sectors' disbursement functions. In order to take account of changes in interest rates, it would be necessary to make considerable refinements in our analysis,

---

perfect substitutability in production, it is possible to relax the assumption of rigid prices. Cf. Leontief, *The Structure of American Economy*, Part II.

which would bring us beyond the scope of this work.[17] We therefore make the assumption that either interest rates do not change (liquidity preference schedules being perfectly elastic) or that, if they do change, they have no effect on disbursement functions (consumption as well as investment being interest-inelastic). If these assumptions did not hold in reality, our models would not become inapplicable. Any actual effects of actual changes in interest rates could be treated as exogeneous changes in disbursement functions.

The Government sector of the economy includes regional and municipal as well as national governments. Their disbursement functions will depend upon government policy, that is to say, on the reactions of government disbursements to changes in revenues. Thus, if governments pursue balanced-budget policies, their marginal propensity to spend to Households and Business will be equal to unity, and their marginal propensity to spend to Finance will be equal to zero. If government expenditures are entirely unrelated to their revenues, Government's marginal propensity to spend will be zero. Government's marginal propensity to spend to Households and Business may be between zero and unity, and possibly greater than unity (e. g., if governments, in an "economy wave," react to a fall in tax yields by still further cutting expenditures); it may even be negative (i. e., government expenditures may rise as tax yields fall, and vice versa) if governments pursue policies designed to stabilize income.

IV. THE KEYNESIAN AND CLASSICAL ASSUMPTIONS

In the Keynesian system only the consumption expenditures of Households are completely income-maintaining;[18] their other disbursements are leakages from the income stream. In terms of our model this means that Households' disbursements to Business come back eventually in the form of disbursements from Business to Households, that is, in the form of income; but that Households' disbursements to Finance and Government never return. We may express this by saying that Business'

---

[17] In the final chapter, however, a method is suggested for taking account of changes in prices and interest rates.

[18] I owe this expression to Mr. E. O. Edwards.

"marginal propensity eventually to spend" to Households is equal to unity, and that Finance's and Government's "marginal propensities eventually to spend" to Households are equal to zero.

A sector's *marginal propensity eventually to spend* to another sector—a concept which we borrow from Lange [19]—is the proportion of the changes in its external receipts which are eventually redisbursed to the other sector. The requirement that a sector have a unit marginal propensity to *spend eventually to another sector* does not imply that it must have a unit marginal propensity to *spend to that sector*; all it means is that it must have a unit marginal propensity to *spend*, and that the money it disburses must go into channels through which it eventually passes back to the other sector. For instance, Business may have a unit marginal propensity to spend, part of which may be devoted to internal spending—for intermediate products—and the rest of which may be devoted to direct spending to Households—say for labor. Eventually, however, the money which passes from firm to firm must find its way back to Households, provided that it is not hoarded or destroyed on its way. If there are to be no leakages in the money stream, any other sector

---

[19] The concept of a "marginal propensity to spend eventually" is based on Dr. Lange's concept of a "marginal propensity to spend back" ("The Theory of the Multiplier," p. 233). At Professor Machlup's suggestion I have decided to abandon Lange's terminology, and replace it by the "marginal propensity to spend eventually," for two reasons: first, the phrase "marginal propensity to spend back" may be misleading because it may give one the impression that it refers to the proportion of a change in disbursements at one time to a change in receipts in the previous period, whereas it is actually—like the "full multiplier" (cf. Machlup, "Period Analysis and Multiplier Theory," p. 220)—the proportion of the *eventual* change in disbursements to an initial change in receipts; secondly, the phrase "marginal propensity to spend back" is less appropriate, for our usage, when more than two sectors are involved.

In his dynamic analysis (p. 233), Lange uses the concept of the "other systems' *propensity to spend back*" in such a way as to make it—like the usual concept of a marginal propensity to spend—equivalent to what he would call the "other systems' marginal propensity to spend externally." That is, he implicitly assumes that the "other systems' marginal propensity to spend internally" is zero. This approximation of a marginal propensity to spend eventually by a marginal propensity to spend in the following period, so that the infinite series of spending back is approximated by a single average spending back after a finite period, is exactly the same as Machlup's approximation, which we shall discuss in the next chapter, of an infinite series of transaction periods by an average income period.

to which Business may make disbursements (for example, Government) must also have a unit marginal propensity to spend. Hence if a sector A is to have a unit marginal propensity eventually to spend to a sector B, then sector A, as well as each of the other sectors (apart from B) to which A disburses money, must have a unit marginal propensity to spend; furthermore, there must be some channel through which the money may pass back to B.

Since Finance has a zero marginal propensity to spend, Business must have a zero marginal propensity to spend to Finance if consumption expenditures are to be completely income-maintaining. Likewise, if Government has a zero marginal propensity to spend (i. e., if government expenditures do not depend on revenues), Business must have, in the Keynesian system, a zero marginal propensity to spend to Government (i. e., there can be no corporate income taxes).[20] Firms must then have unit marginal propensities to spend, exclusive of disbursements to Finance and Government. This has been pointed out by Machlup;[21] more recently, it was demonstrated mathematically by Goodwin.[22]

Any disbursement on the part of Households may be described as income-maintaining if the sector to which it is made has a unit marginal propensity to spend eventually to Households. If, however, the sector to which the disbursement is made has a zero marginal propensity to spend eventually to Households, the disbursement may be described as a leakage. In terms of our model, therefore, the Keynesian assumption is that Households' disbursements to themselves and to Business are income-maintaining, whereas their other disbursements are leakages.

In the Classical system, all disbursements are income-maintaining; this is the requirement of Say's Law.[23] Government,

---

[20] It is surprising that this defect in the Keynesian system should have received so little attention. It may be remedied by the use of a marginal propensity to spend which is smaller than the marginal propensity to consume. See p. 35 n., below.

[21] " Period Analysis and Multiplier Theory," p. 228.

[22] " The Multiplier as Matrix," pp. 542-543.

[23] Cf. Oscar Lange, " Say's Law: A Restatement and Criticism," *Studies in Mathematical Economics and Econometrics,* In Memory of Henry Schultz, edited by Lange, McIntyre and Yntema (Chicago, 1942). Goodwin calls this " Say's

as well as Business, has a unit marginal propensity eventually to spend to Households in the Classical system; that is, governments maintain balanced budgets. Say's Law requires also that savings be income-maintaining; this is made possible in the Classical system by means of the zero interest-elasticity of liquidity preference schedules, which requires all savings to be invested.[24]

In our model we retain the Keynesian assumptions of perfectly elastic liquidity preference schedules; all savings are considered as leakages. We need not, however, regard other Household disbursements either as completely income-maintaining or as leakages. The marginal propensities of Business and Government to spend eventually to Households may be different from zero or unity. In actuality we may expect Business' marginal propensity to spend eventually to Households to be different from unity; this will be so if changes in firms' sales are followed by changes in their debt or cash balances. For instance, firms may increase their indebtedness (or deplete their cash balances) as sales rise, in order to finance new investment; or, if they are burdened with excess inventory (as in early depression) they may use the proceeds of increased sales of durable goods (disinvestment in inventory) to retire debt outstanding. The proportion of changes in business debt and cash balances to Business' sales to Households, multiplied by Households' marginal propensity to spend to Business, is commonly referred to as the marginal propensity to invest.[25] Business' marginal propensity to spend eventually to House-

Law of the Second Kind" ("The Multiplier as Matrix," p. 540). For what Goodwin calls "Say's Law of the First Kind" Lange has used the expression, now widely accepted, "Walras' Law," ("Say's Law," p. 50).

[24] Cf. Oscar Lange, "The Rate of Interest and the Optimum Propensity to Consume," Economica, V (New Series), No. 17 (February, 1938), reprinted in Readings in Business Cycle Theory, p. 177.

[25] If dI/dY is the marginal propensity to invest, we may write $dI/dY = dI/dC_B \cdot dC_B/dY$, where C_B is Households' consumption of goods and services supplied by Business. Therefore the marginal propensity to invest is equal to the proportion of changes in investment to changes in business sales (dI/dC_B) multiplied by the marginal propensity to consume the products of Business (dC_B/dY).

Since, as we shall show in the Appendix to this chapter, Business' external balance is sometimes not investment, but dissaving, the above proportion may in some cases be a marginal propensity to dissave, or a combination of a marginal propensity to dissave and a marginal propensity to invest.

holds will be less than unity to the extent that the business taxes it pays to Government are not returned by Government into the income stream. Government, likewise, may have a marginal propensity to spend eventually to Households which is different from zero or unity.

Appendix to Chapter 2

The Classification of Saving and Investment [26]

We stated in Section II of this chapter that the external balance of the Household and Business sectors was savings and investment, respectively. We may now analyze this proposition more closely.

Investment, or capital outlay, is the difference between Business' total outlay and its current outlay. Business' external balance, on the other hand (its balance of payments exclusive of evidence of debt), is the difference between its total outlay and its receipts. Investment, by this definition, is equivalent to the external balance of Business only if current outlays are equal to receipts. What meaning, then, is to be ascribed to current surpluses or deficits, that is, to the discrepancy, if any, between current outlays and receipts?

A simple example will bring out the meaning of this discrepancy. Let us consider an economy of fishermen, in which fish are the only consumers' goods. Let us imagine, also, that there is an enterprise which hires the fishermen to produce fish, and then sells the fish back to them; and let us assume that all profits, as well as wages, are paid out to the fishermen (that is, the fishermen are capitalists as well as workers). If this economy is in a stationary state, the fishermen will spend all their income on the fish they have produced, so that the enterprise has no capital outlays and no debt; the enterprise will have a zero external balance.

Now suppose the enterprise has a negative external balance. We may distinguish three situations in which this may be the case.

---

[26] The subject-matter of this appendix is also discussed by Leontief in *The Structure of American Economy*, pp. 18-19, 26-27, 29, 42.

(1) The enterprise decides to hire some of the fishermen to produce new capital equipment (nets, boats, etc.), and induces the fishermen to save the appropriate proportion of their income (say by raising the rate of interest); then the current outlays (remuneration of fishermen who are catching fish) are equal to the receipts (sales of fish), whilst the capital outlays (remuneration of fishermen who are producing capital equipment) are financed by borrowing the fishermen's savings. This is a clear case in which the negative external balance is equivalent to investment.

(2) After having been in a stationary state, the fishermen now decide to save part of their income, but still spend all their working time catching fish. As a result, their purchases will fall short of their produce, and one of two things (or a combination of both) must happen: either (a) there is an inventory accumulation of unsold fish, or (b) there is a fall in the price of fish and all the fish are sold. In either case the value of sales falls short of the enterprise's current outlays, and the difference must be financed by borrowing the fishermen's savings. In case 2a, the borrowing finances investment in inventory, and in case 2b it finances a business loss due to a fall in the price of fish. In real terms, the fishermen are lending fish to the enterprise for storage in case 2a, and in case 2b they are lending to the enterprise the excess of the cost of the fish over what they are willing to pay for them.

A positive external balance may be analyzed in a similar fashion. When applied to an enterprise it can again mean three things. (1) There is consumption of capital (through a failure for instance, to replace outworn equipment), so that total outlays are smaller than receipts. In order to maintain consumption, the fishermen borrow from the enterprise. Its positive external balance represents lending from the enterprise to the fishermen to finance the disinvestment. (2) Fishermen consume more than the amount of their income, the discrepancy being reflected in either (a) inventory disinvestment or (b) a rise in the price of fish. In case 2a the enterprise is lending fish from its storehouse to the fishermen, and in case 2b the enterprise is lending money to the fishermen to enable them to pay more for the fish than what they have cost.

In case 1 of both these instances, receipts and current outlays are the same; consequently in the first instance the enterprise's negative external balance is equivalent to investment in new capital equipment, and in the second instance the positive external balance is equivalent to disinvestment, or consumption of capital. In case 2, on the other hand, receipts and current outlays are not the same. In case 2a, the excess of current outlays over receipts is investment in inventory, or an excess of receipts over current outlays is disinvestment in inventory. Consequently the enterprise's external balance is, in case 2a as well as in case 1, investment if the external balance is negative and disinvestment if the external balance is positive. Likewise the fishermen's external balance is savings if it is positive, and dissavings if it is negative.

In case 2b, the fishermen's external balance is still savings if positive, and dissavings if negative. But that part of the enterprise's external balance which consists of the difference between receipts and current outlays is not reflected in investment of any sort, but is simply a business gain, if positive, or a business loss, if negative. Since *ex post* savings and investment must be equal, it follows that these business gains and losses must be classified as saving and dissaving respectively.[27]

This peculiar case 2b is a case of "money illusion." In the first instance the fishermen are willing to save part of their money income, but are not prepared to undertake any saving in real terms (to forego the consumption of fish). There is thus no real saving in the economy; the saving of the fishermen is offset by the dissaving of the enterprise. Likewise, in the second instance the fishermen wish to spend more than the amount of their money income, yet have to be satisfied to consume the same amount of fish as before; here their dissaving is offset by saving on the part of the enterprise.

Any general tendency in the economy towards current deficits or current surpluses that is not reflected in inventory investment or disinvestment, is evidence of money illusion, and must be classified as dissaving or saving, respectively; and to the

[27] This was pointed out to me by Professor Machlup. This differs from the peculiar definition given by Professor Leontief (*The Structure of American Economy*, p. 42), in which a sector's external balance is defined as saving if it is positive and investment if it is negative.

extent that some firms' current surpluses are offset by other firms' current deficits, and to the extent that these current surpluses and deficits are not reflected in inventory changes, there is net lending from firms with surpluses to firms with deficits, which in real terms is a kind of transfer payment or subsidy from profitable to unprofitable firms.

CHAPTER 3

APPLYING THE MODEL

While there are many phenomena which cannot be taken into account in our analysis, it is possible, by means of certain devices, to increase the applicability of the two postulates which govern our system. In this chapter we shall set forth these devices, and indicate the manner in which our analysis may most usefully be applied.

I. APPLICATION OF THE FIRST POSTULATE

The first postulate of our system, it will be recalled, states that each sector's disbursements to every sector are a linear function of that sector's total receipts. We have already noted, in the previous chapter, that there are some cases in which this postulate does not seem to be applicable, for example if loan receipts are, as we suppose, a function of a sector's non-loan receipts. This problem was handled by means of treating such receipts as negative disbursements.

There are other cases, however, in which the functional relationship of some receipts to others cannot be handled so readily in this fashion. Such is the case in which the receipt by Households of transfer payments from Government, say, unemployment insurance benefits, are a negative function of Households' earned receipts. For, assuming that employment and income are closely related, as income rises unemployment insurance payments will fall, and vice versa. This could be dealt with by treating the transfer payment as a negative tax; but in using this device, it would have to be assumed that Households plan their disbursements in relation to their earned receipts only. When we assume that tax payments are a function of total income (total non-loan receipts of Households), it is taken for granted that taxpayers know how much will be taken from them in taxes for any given level of income, so that they can plan their other disbursements accordingly. We cannot in fact make the same psychological assumption with

40

regard to the payment of unemployment insurance benefits; however, such an artificial assumption may serve as an approximation to reality.

An alternative treatment of this problem, however, is possible. It is possible to regard the unemployment insurance fund as a fund of idle balances or hoards: workers contribute to this fund in proportion to their income (this may be regarded as hoarding); they increase their withdrawals from the fund as income falls, and reduce their withdrawals from the fund as income rises.

There is a further pair of devices which is capable of increasing the applicability of our first postulate. Not all the receipts of a sector may be spent in the same way. The same individual may spend his salary and his dividend receipts in different ways; if so, these receipts may be distinguished, and the individual may, for our purposes, be divided into two parts—salary recipient and dividend recipient. Further, many transactions are made through intermediaries, so that a proportion of a sector's receipts may be essentially transient and earmarked for another sector. The payments of consumption taxes from Households to Business, for example, are earmarked for Government; they should therefore be treated either as paid directly to Government, or paid to a special department or collecting agency of Business which in turn remits them to Government. This principle, according to which receipts which are earmarked for a certain sector are considered as paid directly to that sector or to a special collecting agency which remits them to that sector, and according to which receipts which are earmarked for disbursement in different ways are considered as received by separate sectors (or separate departments or collecting agencies of the same sector), may be called the *principle of earmarking*. In general, whenever a sector's disbursement function is different for receipts received for different reasons or from different sources, the sector may be considered as divided into as many different parts as there are different modes of receipt.

II. Analysis of Lags in Money Flows

We saw in the last chapter (Section IV) that a disbursement from Households to another sector is a leakage if that sector has a zero marginal propensity to spend eventually to Households, while it is an income-maintaining disbursement if that sector has a unit marginal propensity to spend eventually to Households. A sector may have a unit marginal propensity to spend eventually to Households either if it disburses all its receipts to Households at once, or if it disburses all its receipts, but some of them internally or to sectors other than Households, so that it takes many rounds of payments before the money finally flows back into the hands of Households. It is therefore necessary to analyze the lags in money flows.

We have made the basic assumption that there is a uniform time lag of disbursements behind receipts for every sector of the economy.[1] This lag of disbursements behind receipts has been called by Professor Machlup the *transaction period*.[2] Aggregative multiplier analysis, on the other hand, assumes in its dynamic formulation that there is a uniform *income-propagation period*. The latter is defined by Professor Machlup as " the length of time which it takes for the money in active circulation to complete a circuit flow from income recipient to income recipient." [3] In actuality, Households' disbursements to other sectors will return into the income stream at different periods of time, rather than simultaneously; consequently, the income period is an average of a " varied number of transaction periods of varied length." [4]

Aggregative dynamic multiplier analysis postulates, as an empirical approximation to reality, an economy in which there is an income-propagation period of uniform length. Ignoring Finance and Government (since disbursements to these sectors are considered in Keynesian multiplier analysis to be leakages), we may set up an economy consisting of Households and

---

[1] In the following section, however, we shall introduce a device which enables us to deal with unequal time lags.
[2] " Period Analysis and Multiplier Theory," p. 204.
[3] *Ibid.*, p. 208.
[4] *Ibid.*, p. 212.

Business, each with a zero marginal propensity to spend internally, indicating that there is no interpersonal spending in Households, or that any such interpersonal spending is regarded as done through Business; and that there are no inter-firm transactions, that is, that the Business sector is a giant, vertically-integrated firm—or alternatively, inter-firm transactions occur without any lag at all. Furthermore it is assumed that Business has a unit marginal propensity to spend to Households (so that all disbursements to Business are completely income-maintaining), and that Households have a marginal propensity to spend to Business equal to the marginal propensity to consume. The sum of the lag between Households' receipts from and disbursements to Business (Households' transaction period) and the lag between Business' receipts from and disbursements to Households (Business' transaction period) is the income-propagation period. In this way, the lags in inter-firm transactions are not ignored but are averaged out into a single income period.

In actuality, the spending of certain funds from Business back to Households occurs not as a discrete payment but in an infinite series of installments which finally become negligible. This whole structure of installments, derived from firms' disbursement functions, and made up of payments in intervals of transaction periods, is approximated in aggregative dynamic multiplier analysis by one single payment made after an average interval which is the income-propagation period.

In this "Machlup sequence," as it may be called, there is a lag between Households' receipts and Households' disbursements to Business, and a further lag between Households' disbursements to Business and Business' redisbursements to Households. It is sometimes assumed in the economic literature that only one of these lags exists. The assumption that Households disburse their receipts with a lag whereas Business disburses its receipts without lag has been described by Dr. Metzler as the assumption of the "expenditure lag" or "Robertsonian sequence"; and the assumption that Households disburse their receipts without lag whereas Business disburses its receipts back to Households with one lag, has been described as the assumption of the "output lag" or "Lundberg sequence."[5] It is quite possible, however, for simple aggregative dynamic multiplier analysis to deal with both of these lags, combined into the Machlup sequence.

The weakness of aggregative dynamic multiplier analysis, as Professor Goodwin has pointed out,[6] lies in its approximation of the distributed lag[7] of transaction periods by a single income period. Matrix-multiplier analysis, according to Goodwin, can take account of this distributed lag by dealing with a multi-sector economy in which each sector has a uniform transaction period.[8] Yet, in so setting up a model in which equal transaction periods are assumed, matrix-multiplier analysis may not be any more realistic than simple-multiplier analysis. For example, there may be very great discrepancies between lag, behind a firm's receipts, of its payments of wages and its payments for new capital equipment, and among the lags of its payments for different kinds of materials. Though a transaction period is more meaningful than an income period, and has a greater qualitative significance—owing to the fact that an income period is a concept of approximation to a distributed lag made up of a number of transaction periods—it is nevertheless possible that, quantitatively, the assumption of equal income periods is closer to reality than the assumption of equal transaction periods. This is what the Cambridge school would contend in its preference for the concept of income velocity rather than transactions velocity. (This was pointed out to me by Professor Machlup.) It is probably the most appropriate procedure to analyze the economy in terms of transaction periods rather than in terms of income periods, but to take account, at the same time, of the discrepancies among transaction periods.

---

[5] Lloyd A. Metzler, "Three Lags in the Circular Flow of Income," *Income, Employment, and Public Policy, Essays in Honor of Alvin Hansen* (New York, 1948), pp. 11-32.

[6] "The Multiplier as Matrix," p. 553.

[7] A "distributed lag" may be defined as a (finite or infinite) set of (weighted) chronologically ordered intervals of time each receding from a given date. This was suggested to me by Dr. William C. Hood.

[8] It should be noted here that a simple two-sector economy (Households and Business) can deal with the assumption of equal transaction periods. The desirability of further subdivision arises out of differences in firms' disbursement functions.

III. Application of the Second Postulate

We may now introduce a device which can take account of differences in transaction periods, and thus enable us to give realism to our second postulate that there is a definite, uniform transaction period throughout the economy.

If the lag between a sector i's receipts and its disbursements to sector j is twice as long, for instance, as the lag between its receipts and its disbursements to sector k, then we may simply pretend that there exists a certain collecting agency l, through which the money passes on its way from i to j. Thus the payment from i to j may be regarded as split up into a payment from i to l over one period (i's marginal propensity

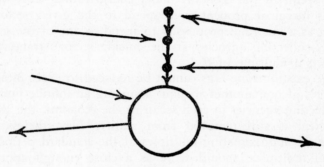

Figure 2.

to spend to l being, in fact, i's marginal propensity to spend to j), and a payment from l to j in the following period (l's marginal propensity to spend to j being equal to unity). In this way we may insert into the economy as many goblins as we please whose sole function is to obey Say's Law and hold up the flow of money!

For practical purposes it may be desirable to assume a minimum number of different transaction periods. Let these transaction periods all be integral multiples of a certain *standard period*. If the length of this standard period is θ, and if the r transaction periods are (or approximate) integral multiples of θ up to $r\theta$, and if the economy is divided into n sectors, then at most $(r-1)n$ collecting agencies will be inserted into the economy. This may be shown in a simple diagram (Figure 2) where the circle represents any sector of the economy, and each dot represents a collecting agency. The large arrows represent inflows of money from other sectors, and outflows to other sectors or their respective collecting agencies. Depending upon whether inflows come directly or through one or more collecting agencies, the transaction period will be shorter or longer.[9] In this example, there are four transaction periods—θ, 2θ, 3θ and 4θ—and each sector must therefore have at most three collecting agencies. The third collecting agency has a unit marginal propensity to spend to the second, the second has a unit marginal propensity to spend to the first, and the first a unit marginal propensity to spend to the sector of the economy under consideration. Any other sector's marginal propensity to spend to the given sector is treated as a marginal propensity to spend to one of the given sector's collecting agencies, if the outside sector's transaction period is a multiple of θ.

Since existing time lags cannot be reduced to exact integral multiples of one another without assigning an infinite number of collecting agencies to each sector of the economy, the above refinement is still removed from reality. Nevertheless our scheme, in approximating multiples of the standard period by integral multiples, should serve as a close enough approximation to reality to suffice for practical purposes.

It is suggestive, now that we have introduced our new device, to think of the transaction period in the same way as we previously considered the income period. In the case of the income period we singled out receivers of income (Households) from other sectors, and applied Machlup's definition: "the length of time which it takes for the money in active circulation to complete a circuit flow from income recipient to income recipient." We may define the transaction period in the same way by singling out receivers of (genuine) commodity transactions and donations (Households, Business and Government— we do not include financial transactions) from other participants

---

[9] Though we make the supposition that goblins, as well as sectors, are "transactors" (illicit transactors, we may call them), the term "transaction period" must still be reserved for the lag in payments among *genuine* transactors.

(goblins), and extrapolating Machlup's definition, to read: "the length of time which it takes for the money in active circulation to complete a circuit flow from transactor [10] to transactor." [10] In the same way that the income period is an average of a distributed lag of transaction periods, so is the transaction period an average of a distributed lag of standard periods.

IV. ON THE APPLICATION OF THE MODEL AS A WHOLE

Conceptually, the economy may be divided, for the purpose of our analysis, into all its component organisms. There are good reasons, however, for not going to this extreme of dissection. What are the manner in which, and the degree to which, the economy may be most usefully divided for the various purposes for which our analysis may be used?

Functional and Regional Divisions

We may first discuss the alternative ways in which the economy may be divided. The two main criteria according to which the division may be made are functional and regional.

In a functional division, it is possible to take into account all four principal sectors (and subdivisions thereof), or to consider a sector or group of sectors in isolation. It is quite possible, for instance, to use a Government-Households model, a Business-Households model, a Households-Finance model, and so on. In a simple Government-Households model, for example, Household disbursements to Business which are redisbursed to Government may be regarded as Household disbursements to Government, and Household disbursements to Business which are eventually redisbursed to Households may be treated as intra-Household disbursements; in this way, sectors which are apparently left out of the model are implicitly taken into account. A distortion, it must always be remembered, is made in such models with regard to time lags; each model will have an appropriate average propagation period relevant to it. In a Business-Households model in which Government has a zero marginal propensity to spend, the appropriate lag is the trans-

---

[10] This word is to be understood here to mean the Households, Business, and Government sectors, and to exclude Finance and collecting agencies.

action period; if Government has a non-zero marginal propensity to spend, the appropriate lag will be longer in order to take account of the indirect disbursements between Business and Households, and within Business and Households, through Government. In a Government-Households model the lag will be an average of the income period (Households' lag) and the lag of government expenditures behind government revenues. In general, the appropriate lag in any model is, to extrapolate Machlup's definition, "the average length of time which it takes for the money in active circulation to complete a circuit flow from participator to participator," where a participator is a sector which is explicitly included in the model.

We have seen how, as Professor Goodwin pointed out, Keynesian economics can isolate the Households sector from the rest of the economy. It does so by adjusting Households' marginal propensities to spend to other sectors by weighting them by the other sectors' marginal propensities eventually to spend to Households. In the strictly Keynesian case, the weight applied to Households' marginal propensity to spend to Business is equal to unity (if Say's Law applies to Business), and the weights applied to Households' marginal propensities to spend to other sectors is equal to zero. If Say's Law does not apply to Business it is quite possible (and indeed, has been done) to adjust Households' marginal propensity to spend to Business by a weight other than unity, to wit, by the introduction of the concept of a marginal propensity to invest. We also saw how, dynamically, the Keynesian isolation of Households is accomplished by means of the concept of the income-propagation period. It is equally possible to study any other sector of the economy, such as Business, in isolation, by making the appropriate adjustments (according to other sectors' marginal propensities eventually to spend to Business) in Business' marginal propensities to spend, and by deriving the relevant average propagation period. It is even possible, in this way, to isolate a single industry or firm, or a region or country.

The second criterion according to which the economy may be divided is the regional one. There are numerous factors which combine to make for regional differences in the disbursement functions of economic organisms. One such factor is the existence of artificial barriers, such as tariffs, immigration barriers, fluctuating exchange rates, and governmental direction of trade among nations. Because of the intensity of these barriers, countries are natural economic groups with which to deal. A certain number of artificial barriers (customs unions, intergovernmental agreements, etc.) may also make it convenient to group together a number of countries; thus groups like "Western Europe" and "Latin America" may form meaningful agglomerations for certain purposes. Likewise the states or provinces in a federally organized nation may have a sufficient degree of independence to make it desirable to distinguish among them.

In addition to artificial barriers, there are many natural barriers which make it advisable to divide the economy into geographical areas. Regional differences in the degree of industrialization, regional specialization, immobility of labor among different areas, and a host of social and cultural differences from region to region, all make for geographical heterogeneity of disbursement functions.[11]

A regional division of particular interest is that of "advanced" and "backward" regions. Many of the factors mentioned above may combine to delineate these two categories. The advanced region may be a country, or a closely knit group of countries, or a relatively independent province or state within a country; it may also be an industrial area, and a region marked off by special social and cultural characteristics. Similarly, the backward region may be a closely knit continent, a country, or a province or a state, and it may also be a region characterized by agriculture and extractive industries, and distinguished by marked social and cultural differences. One would expect, for instance, that Say's Law would be more likely to rule in an undeveloped area than in a mature one. One will sometimes find, also, that a "mature" economy is relatively self-sufficient whereas an "immature" one is subject to severe "regional leakages"; thus, a large proportion of a

[11] For a discussion of the concept of an economic region, cf. Rutledge Vining, "Location of Industry and Regional Patterns of Business Cycle Behavior" and "The Region as a Concept in Business-Cycle Analysis," *Econometrica*, Vol. 14, Nos. 1 & 3 (January and July, 1946), pp. 37-68 and 201-218.

rise in a backward area's income may leak out to an advanced area in the form of dividends and imports of manufactured goods.

Though it is theoretically possible to group sectors completely along regional lines, it is unwise to do so, since there is not sufficient homogeneity among the organisms within a region. If we exclude Finance from the model in all regions (which we can do since Finance has a zero marginal propensity to spend) and assume that all other sectors have equal marginal propensities to spend [12] and equal transaction periods, we may aggregate these sectors together and analyze interregional money flows.[13] A procedure of this kind may be helpful to the understanding of the phenomena involved, but it is not to be recommended on any other grounds. It is preferable, then, either to make a functional subdivision of the regions, or to isolate the Households sector in each region. We shall return, after the following digression, to a discussion of the latter procedure.

A Digression on Types of Equilibrium

We may profitably digress, at this point, to consider the three types of equilibrium that correspond to the alternative ways of analyzing the multi-sector economy. These three types may be called partial-equilibrium, general-equilibrium, and full-equilibrium analysis. An analysis which isolates a sector in such a way as to assume that its behavior affects the other sectors in such a negligible degree that it brings forth no repercussions to itself, is partial-equilibrium analysis. An analysis which, on the contrary, takes account of all sectors and of the interrelationships among them, is general-equilibrium analysis. An analysis which takes account of one sector or aggregation of sectors, and makes adjustments for repercussions brought about by its interaction with other sectors, may be called full-equilibrium analysis.

[12] This includes organisms' marginal propensities to pay taxes. If Government has a zero marginal propensity to spend, we may exclude governments from the model, in which case only the Business and Household sectors are aggregated, and taxes are not included in the marginal propensity to spend.
[13] These money flows will be commodity transactions and donations. If governments are excluded (see note 12), donations will not be included in the money flows, since non-governmental donations may safely be ignored.

Mathematically, the disbursement function of a single sector—the array of its disbursements to every sector expressed as a function of its receipts—may be regarded as a set of partial-equilibrium equations, since it shows the amount of disbursements throughout the economy which are due to variations in its receipts alone; the system of equations as a whole, which describes the interrelationship among all the sectors of the economy, is a system of general equilibrium; and the solutions of this system of equations are a set of full-equilibrium equations. Full-equilibrium analysis proceeds directly to the solved form, rather than through the parameters of the general equilibrium equations. The Keynesian procedure of isolating the Households sector of the economy and adjusting its marginal propensities to spend by other sectors' marginal propensities eventually to spend to Households, employs the full-equilibrium approach.[14]

The term "general equilibrium" is customarily used to describe the interrelationship among economic organisms, and the term "microeconomics" is used to denote the partial-equilibrium analysis of such organisms. The term "macroeconomics" refers to the kind of theory which pictures the economy as an aggregation of economic organisms. Professor Leontief has described his theory as a general-equilibrium one. Accordingly, we may describe by the term "*pure* general equilibrium" the kind of analysis used in the theories of Walras, Pareto, and Cassel, and employ, for a system of interrelated groups or partial aggregates, the term "*aggregative* general equilibrium."

Intrasectoral Equilibrium Analysis

Just as it is possible, by using the full-equilibrium approach, to deal with one sector in isolation without neglecting reper-

---

[14] If we are to accept Professor Friedman's interpretation of Marshall (cf. Milton Friedman, "The Marshallian Demand Curve," *Journal of Political Economy*, LVII [December, 1949]), according to which the demand curve is defined in such a way that real income is assumed constant and other prices rise as the given price falls, then Marshallian equilibrium, like Keynesian aggregative equilibrium, is a form of full equilibrium. Such a demand curve may be *derived* from the Walrasian system by reducing the general equilibrium equations to the solved form; but Marshall prefers to start with the solved form from the outset.

cussions from the outside, it is also possible to deal with the interrelationships among the subdivisions of any sector. Thus, we may analyze interrelationships among subdivisions of Business (such as, for example, the Marxian departments—consumers' goods industry and producers' goods industry), and the interrelationships among subdivisions of Households (such as classes or regions). The traditional foreign-trade multiplier analysis is one of the latter sort: it retains the Keynesian isolation of Households, and analyzes the interrelationships between the national incomes (Household receipts) of two countries. It retains, therefore, the Keynesian assumptions with regard to other sectors' marginal propensities to spend eventually to Households (except insofar as the concept of a marginal propensity to invest is introduced [15]), and the assumption of equal average income-propagation periods.

The analysis of intra-Household income movements partakes partly of (aggregative) general-equilibrium analysis and partly of full-equilibrium analysis. It is a general-equilibrium analysis to the extent that it examines the interdependence of and interrelationships among regions or among classes of the population; it is full-equilibrium analysis to the extent that the parameters involved (the marginal propensities of regions or classes to spend to themselves and to each other) are derived from the regions' or classes' marginal propensities to spend to sectors which are not explicitly taken into consideration, and from these sectors' marginal propensities to spend eventually to the regions or classes. A region's marginal propensity to spend to another region—more accurately, the derived marginal propensity of a region's Household sector to spend to another region's Household sector—is equal to that region's marginal propensities to spend to Business and Government, respectively multiplied by Business' and Government's marginal propensities to spend their receipts eventually to the other region. Similarly, workers' marginal propensity to spend to capitalists is—apart from direct interpersonal disbursements—equal to workers' marginal propensities to spend to Business and Government, respec-

[15] Cf. Lloyd A. Metzler, "Underemployment Equilibrium in International Trade"; also, "The Transfer Problem Reconsidered," *Journal of Political Economy*, L (June, 1942), reprinted in *Readings in the Theory of International Trade* (Philadelphia, 1949).

tively multiplied by Business' and Government's marginal propensities to spend their receipts eventually to capitalists.

The assumption of equal income-propagation periods in the regional multiplier may be expected to be considerably less realistic than in the case of the simple aggregative multiplier, for the lag between Household receipts and Household receipts for one region may be shorter than the lag between its Household receipts and the Household receipts of a distant region. The reverse may also be true; a rise in disbursements in a coal-producing region will affect the Household receipts of a region producing finished goods more rapidly than its own Household receipts. There is also considerable distortion in the assumption of equal income-propagation periods in the analysis of inter-class income movements; for the average lag between Business receipts and the payment of profits is much larger than the average lag between Business receipts and the payment of wages. Full-equilibrium analysis, while useful for many purposes and valuable in its simplicity, may lead to treacherous distortions of reality in dynamical theory.

The application of aggregative general-equilibrium analysis to the problems of regionalism and income distribution requires explicit inclusion of Business and Government. Since these sectors are so heterogeneous in nature, subdivisions of them will also be necessary. To the extent that transaction periods differ markedly, collecting agencies must be inserted to allow for the discrepancy.

The Optimum Degree of Division

The degree to which the economy should be divided for analysis depends upon a large number of considerations, especially, of course, the particular problem at hand. A basic factor which should always be taken into account is the degree of heterogeneity of the various sectors of the economy. By nature, disbursement functions of firms vary widely; consequently, Business' disbursement function will differ for autonomous disbursement in different industries. An autonomous expansion in the steel industry, for instance, will have an effect different from that of an autonomous expansion of the same amount in the textile industry, because of the widely differing manner in which the disbursements channel their way through the economy. Likewise, autonomous disbursements that accrue more to capitalists than to workers will have different multiplying effects on all sectors' receipts from those which accrue more to workers.

It should not be supposed, however, that on account of the heterogeneity of different parts of the economy, the dissection should be carried out to the maximum extent. There are many important factors making for diminishing returns to subdivision.

Differences in the marginal propensities to spend of different economic organisms are of two sorts: non-random and random. To the extent that differences among economic organisms' marginal propensities to spend are non-random, these organisms may be described as heterogeneous in this respect; they may be called homogeneous to the extent that these differences are purely random. The disaggregation of a heterogeneous group or sector into a number of homogeneous groups will tend to increase the stability of the parameters (the marginal propensities to spend). On the other hand, the disaggregation of a homogeneous group into smaller groups will not increase the stability of the parameters; in fact, such disaggregation, beyond a certain point, will reduce the stability of the parameters, owing to the law of large numbers. Diminishing returns to subdivision set in when the disaggregation is carried out beyond the point where differences among organisms' marginal propensities to spend partake more and more of a random nature.

Thus it is clearly an advantage, from this standpoint, to distinguish among individuals belonging to different classes or income-groups, or residing in different regions, and among firms belonging to different industries.[16]

In addition to differences in the properties of organisms, differences in the properties of commodities will also influence the optimum degree to which the economy should be divided. The greater the extent to which the disaggregation is carried out, the larger will be the number of sectors to which each sector will have a separate marginal propensity to spend. If

[16] Cairnes' " non-competing groups " fit very well into these categories, as has been suggested to me by Professor Donald B. Marsh. Cf. Cairnes, *Some Leading Principles of Political Economy*, pp. 290-294. Cf. also Bastable, *Theory of International Trade*, Chapter I, pp. 31-32, 103-104.

commodities or groups of commodities are complementary with one another, a sector's marginal propensity to buy any of these commodities will tend to be relatively stable; on the other hand, a sector's marginal propensity to buy individual commodities or groups of commodities will tend to be unstable if they are relatively substitutable for one another. Thus the marginal propensity to buy food or to buy housing is more stable than the marginal propensity to buy a particular kind of food or a particular kind of housing.

There is a further sense, therefore, in which sectors may be said to be homogeneous or heterogeneous: a group of organisms is relatively homogeneous or heterogeneous in this sense if the products of these organisms are respectively relatively substitutable for one another or relatively complementary with one another, from the point of view of other sectors. If a group of organisms is heterogeneous with respect to these organisms' marginal propensities to spend, it is quite possible for the products of these organisms to be substitutable for one another; if this is so, the division of this heterogeneous group into homogeneous groups will reduce the stability of *other* groups' marginal propensities to spend. For instance, the division of the meat industry into the beef industry and the pork industry will reduce the stability of consumers' marginal propensities to spend, since the marginal propensities to buy beef and to buy pork will be less stable, taken separately, than the marginal propensity to buy meat.

Whenever substitutability is present, there will be a tendency for the components of a sector's marginal propensity to spend to fluctuate in opposite directions and cancel each other out. As commodities are broken down into finer and finer categories, the substitutability among these categories may be expected to increase, with the result that the marginal propensity to buy any particular commodity or group of commodities will be less stable than the marginal propensity to buy a broad class of commodities. This is especially true in regional analysis, since the existence of alternative sources of supply from different regions makes the regions' marginal propensities to spend to one another highly variable and unstable if the regions are too small.[17] There is therefore a zone within which it may not be possible to increase the stability of some parameters without decreasing the stability of others. Hence a certain amount of disaggregation of sectors producing substitutable commodities and aggregation of sectors with different marginal propensities to spend may be unavoidable.

The degree of substitutability among commodity groups varies with the degree and mode of division of commodities into commodity groups. To the extent that, under a given degree of division, the degree of substitutability among commodity groups is large, the law of large numbers will operate. The law of large numbers and the tendency towards heterogeneity work in contrary directions; in between the points of complete decomposition and complete aggregation, an optimum degree of division exists which maximizes the stability of the parameters.

A further factor which must be taken into consideration in deciding upon the optimum degree of division of the economy is the possibility and accuracy of statistical estimation of the parameters. In some cases, the availability and reliability of statistical estimates may decline markedly with the degree of subdivision. This is particularly true in the case of interregional analysis; while international data are available, there are, in most countries, no interregional trade data.[18] This gives rise to serious difficulties which cannot easily be surmounted.[19]

Next, the computational difficulties must be borne in mind. As the number of sectors increases, difficulties of computation mount rapidly to the point where the calculation is, as Professor Goodwin has said, " [removed] from the sphere of the ordinary economist." [20] Fortunately, however, the handling of hundreds of equations is no longer an impossible problem; it is only the

[17] The existence of alternative sources of supply may also give rise to discontinuity in regional disbursement functions; that is, as a region's income rises its imports may, at a certain point, shift entirely from one source to another. This was pointed out to me by Professor Tjalling C. Koopmans.

[18] In some countries there are not even any regional income data.

[19] It may be possible to derive approximations to the parameters by means of Professor Sargant Florence's " location factor." Cf. Rutledge Vining, " Location of Industry and Regional Patterns of Business-Cycle Behavior," *Econometrica*, Vol. 14, No. 1, pp. 37-68.

[20] "The Multiplier as Matrix," p. 544.

expense of calculation involved which is a computational impediment to extreme subdivision.

Finally, we must consider the effect of the inequality of time lags. If all economic organisms are involved explicitly in the analysis, so that the relevant period is the transaction period, inequalities in transaction periods may be remedied, as we saw in the previous section, by the introduction of collecting agencies. If there is considerable discrepancy among transaction periods, a large number of collecting agencies will have to be inserted. Computational difficulties are not greatly affected by the introduction of collecting agencies, for each collecting agency has a unit marginal propensity to spend to one other collecting agency or sector, and a zero marginal propensity to spend to all others. The presence of such a large number of zero terms in each collecting agency's disbursement function adds but little to computational difficulties.

All these considerations must be carefully balanced in order to determine an appropriate degree of division of the economy. In the case of interregional and international trade, where marginal propensities of regions and countries to spend to one another are less technological in nature than are the Leontief coefficients in interindustrial trade, subdivision cannot be carried out as far as it is in the Leontief interindustrial analysis. The regions which are chosen should be fairly large.[21] It may be desirable, in interregional and international analysis, to introduce Business and Government sectors explicitly into the system, and to allow for unequal transaction periods. In this case the subdivision will be more extensive than in full-equilibrium regional anaylsis.

[21] In the case of the United States, the optimum size for a region in full-equilibrium interregional analysis is probably of the order of a Federal Reserve district; in this I have the oral agreement of Professor Werner Hochwald of Washington University in St. Louis. The regional multiplier is particularly valuable in a country with as markedly different regions as Canada; in Canada, the province comes close to being the ideal unit, though groupings of provinces and subdivisions of provinces may be desirable.

PART II

TWO SECTORS

CHAPTER 4

THE BI-SECTOR MULTIPLIER [1]

We shall now develop a static formulation of the multiplier for two sectors. The formulation presented in this chapter is an extension of the Machlup formulation; an equivalent alternative formulation which is more appropriate for extension to the multi-sector multiplier, and which is closer to the Metzler and Lange formulations, will be presented in the next chapter. Since the Machlup formulation is in terms of saving and investment, we shall retain the foreign trade analogy, and speak in terms of "income" and "expenditure" rather than in terms of "receipts" and "disbursements." A graphical method will be introduced into the analysis, and a generalized formulation will be presented of which the formulas presented by Dr. Machlup will be found to be special cases.

I. The Closed Sector Multiplier

The familiar closed sector national income multiplier may be illustrated as in Figure 3. Income (Y) is measured on the abscissa, and savings (S) and investment (I) on the ordinate. Writing $S = S(Y)$ for the savings function and $I = I(Y)$ for the investment function, we have $S' = S'(Y)$ for the marginal propensity to save, and $I' = I'(Y)$ for the marginal propensity to invest. Income (OY_1) is determined by the intersection (A_1) of the savings and investment functions. A rise in the investment function from $I_1(Y)$ to $I_2(Y)$ brings about an increase in income of Y_1Y_2.

The multiplier (k) may be defined in two ways: **(1)** as the increment in income (A_1K) divided by the total increment in investment (A_2K), giving us

[1] This chapter, in slightly different form, appeared in the *Canadian Journal of Economics and Political Science*, XV (May, 1949), under the title "The Generalized Bi-System Multiplier." It is reproduced with the kind permission of the *Canadian Journal* and the University of Toronto Press.

(4. 1)
$$k = \frac{1}{\dfrac{A_2 K}{A_1 K}} = \frac{1}{S'} \; ;$$

and (2) as the increment in income divided by the *autonomous* increment in investment $(A_2 J)$, which gives us

(4. 2)
$$k = \frac{1}{\dfrac{A_2 K}{A_1 K} - \dfrac{JK}{A_1 K}} = \frac{1}{S' - I'}$$

where JK is *induced* investment.

Multipliers (4. 1) and (4. 2) are equivalent only if the marginal propensity to invest is equal to zero; the use of (4. 1) under the second definition therefore requires a restrictive

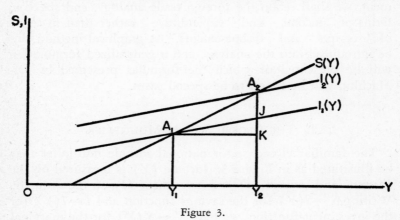

Figure 3.

assumption. (4. 2) may therefore be called the generalized closed sector multiplier. We shall employ the second definition throughout this work.

II. THE OPEN SECTOR MULTIPLIER

In an open sector there are leakages (imports) which leave the economy as well as those (savings) which remain in the sector. We shall use the term open sector multiplier to denote an induced increment in income divided by an autonomous increment in expenditure, in a sector in which leakages which leave the economy do not return.

Let $M = M(Y)$ be the import function, and $X = X(Y)$ the export function. Then $M' = M'(Y)$ is the marginal propensity to import, and $X' = X'(Y)$ is the marginal propensity to export. If the open sector is the private economy, and the external sector is the government, then M' is the marginal propensity to be taxed (determined by the tax structure) and X' is the marginal propensity to receive government expenditure. If, for instance, unemployment insurance benefits increase as income falls, there is a negative marginal propensity to " export."

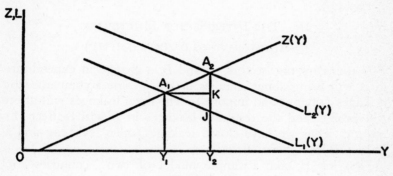

Figure 4.

Let C be the rate of consumption, and E expenditure on the products of the economy, per unit of time. Then $E = C + I + X$, and $Y = C + S + M$. The equilibrium condition $Y = E$ requires the conditions $S - I = X - M$. Write $Z = S - I$, and $L = X - M$, where Z is excess savings, and L is the external balance. Then income is determined, as shown in Figure 4, by the intersection of the excess savings and external balance functions. OY_1 is equilibrium income, and A_1Y_1 is "net foreign lending." If the intersection occurred below the abscissa, A_1Y_1 would represent "net foreign borrowing." If leakages, once they leave the economy, do not return, a rise in the external balance function from $L_1(Y)$ to $L_2(Y)$ increases income according to the multiplier

$$(4.3) \qquad k = \frac{1}{\dfrac{A_1K}{A_2K} + \dfrac{JK}{A_1K}} = \frac{1}{Z' - L'} \ .$$

A change in the excess savings function yields the same multiplier. The open sector multiplier is therefore the reciprocal of the marginal propensity to underspend [2] less the marginal propensity to have a positive external balance.

When the open sector is the private economy, L' represents the marginal propensity to have an external balance with the government. A_1Y_1 in this case represents lending to the government, i. e., the budget deficit. A balanced budget would be represented by the intersection of the curves on the abscissa, and a budget surplus by an intersection below the abscissa.

III. THE INTER-SECTOR MULTIPLIER
(WITH NO SAVINGS OR INVESTMENT)

If there are two sectors, A and B, a change in expenditure in A will bring about changes in A's income accompanied by leakages (savings and imports). The open leakages will affect B's income, and the resulting leakages in B will reaffect A's income. Thus we have closed leakages, open leakages, and a third factor—repercussions.

First let us take a simple model of two "countries" in trade, in neither of which there is any saving or investment. Expenditure then consists only of consumption and exports, and income is devoted only to consumption and imports. Let us first assume that exports are independent of income ($X' = 0$). The equilibrium condition requires that exports equal imports.

In Figure 5, the two sectors are shown in equilibrium. Income in both A and B is determined by the intersection of the import and export functions, and the quantity G_1Y_1 of A's exports and imports is identical with the quantity Q_1Y_1 of B's imports and exports.

Now let there be an autonomous rise in A's exports, shown by an upward shift in A's export function. Since A's exports are identically the same as B's imports, there will be an equal

---

[2] In my original article, "The Generalized Bi-System Multiplier," I used the term "marginal propensity to excess-save." At Professor Machlup's suggestion, I have abandoned this term in favor of the expression "marginal propensity to underspend."

upward shift in B's import function. With the rise in A's exports, A's income will rise and increase A's imports in accordance with A's import function; similarly the fall in B's income following from the rise in its imports will induce a fall in its imports. In accordance with Dr. Machlup's terminology, we shall call these the home-induced changes in imports. Thirdly, there are the foreign-induced changes. A rise in A's exports brings about a rise in A's income; at the same time,

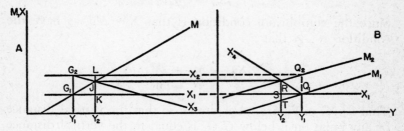

Figure 5.

being a rise in B's imports, it brings about a decline in B's income and consequently in B's imports (which are A's exports). This is a foreign-induced decline in A's exports. Since the rise in A's exports brings about a foreign-induced decline in its exports at the same time as it brings about a rise in its income, we may express foreign-induced exports (B's imports) as a negative function of A's income, as represented by X_3 in Figure 5A.[3] B's foreign-induced export function is similarly represented by X_4 in Figure 5B.

---

[3] Mathematically speaking, the home-induced export and import functions are fundamental relationships, whereas the foreign-induced export function is a derived relationship. In A, as X rises, Y rises, so

$$Y_A = f(X_A).$$

The same rise in exports lowers B's income, so

$$Y_B = g(X_A)$$

B's import function is then

$$M_B = M_B(Y_B) = M_B(g(X_A)) = \phi(X_A)$$

Since Y_A and M_B are both functions of X_A,

$$M_B = \psi(Y_A)$$

as long as $dX_A \neq 0$, which is the case here.

Using the subscripts a, h and f for 'autonomous,' 'home-induced,' and 'foreign-induced,' we have in A:

$$_aX_A$$
$$_hM_A$$
$$- _fX_A = - _hM_B$$

and in B:

$$_aM_B$$
$$- _hM_B$$
$$_fX_B = _hM_A.$$

Since the equilibrium condition is that $X = M$, we have the condition for A that

$$_aX_A - _fX_A = _hM_A$$
$$_aX_A - _hM_B = _hM_A$$
$$X_3 = M.$$

That is, X_3 in Figure 5A is drawn so that the vertical distance of any point on it below G_2Q_2 is equal to the vertical distance of the horizontally opposite point on M_2 below G_2Q_2.[4]

Similarly, in B we have the condition that

$$_aM_B - _hM_B = _fX_B$$
$$= _hM_A$$
$$M_2 = X_4.$$

That is, X_4 in Figure 5B is drawn so that the vertical distance of any point on it below G_2Q_2 is equal to the vertical distance below G_2Q_2 of the horizontally opposite point on M.[4]

The result of a rise in A's exports from X_1 to X_2 is then a movement from the initial equilibrium points G_1 and Q_1 to the new equilibrium points J and R, so that $JY_2 = RY_2$ is the new level of exports and imports, and A's income has risen while B's has fallen.

The multiplier for A (the increment in A's income divided by the autonomous increment in A's exports) is determined as follows:

$$(4.4) \qquad k_A = \frac{G_1K}{LJ + JK} = \frac{1}{\dfrac{LJ}{G_2L} + \dfrac{JK}{G_1K}} = \frac{1}{M'_B + M'_A}.$$

[4] I am indebted to Professor G. A. Elliott for the rewriting of this sentence.

Similarly, for B:

$$k_B = \frac{Q_1 S}{RS + ST} = \frac{1}{\dfrac{RS}{Q_1 S} + \dfrac{ST}{Q_1 S}} = \frac{1}{M'_A + M'_B} .$$

The multiplier in both sectors is equal to the reciprocal of the sum of the two countries' marginal propensities to import. The increased income in A is exactly equal to the decreased income in B.

Let us now consider the case in which exports are income-elastic (Figure 6). Assuming the marginal propensity to export

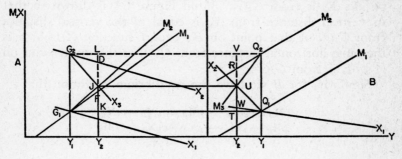

Figure 6.

to be negative, we have the equilibrium level of imports and exports shown by the height of the line $G_1 Q_1$ joining the equilibrium points of A's and B's import and export functions. There are now two additional factors to account for: home-induced changes in exports, and foreign-induced changes in imports. Our classifications of changes in imports and exports are then as follows. For A there are:

$$_a X_A$$
$$_h M_A$$
$$- {_h X_A}$$
$$- {_f X_A} = - {_h M_B}$$
$$_f M_A = {_h X_B}$$

and for B:

$$_a M_B$$
$$- {_h M_B}$$
$$_h X_B$$
$$_f X_B = {_h M_A}$$
$$- {_f M_B} = - {_h X_A} .$$

For A, the equilibrium condition of equality of exports and imports requires that

$$_aX_A - {}_hX_A - {}_fX_A = {}_hM_A + {}_fM_A$$
$$_aX_A - {}_hX_A - {}_hM_B = {}_hM_A + {}_hX_B$$
$$X_3 = M_2.$$

That is, X_3 in Figure 6A is drawn so that the vertical distance of any point on it below X_2 is equal to the vertical distance below G_2Q_2 of that point on B's import function M_2 which is the same horizontal distance from Q_2Q_1 as the given point on A's X_3 is from G_2G_1. M_2 in Figure 6A is drawn so that its vertical distance from M_1 is equal to the vertical distance from G_1Q_1 of that point on B's export function X_1 which is the same horizontal distance from Q_2Q_1 as the given point on A's M_2 is from G_2G_1.

Similarly, for B we have the equilibrium condition that

$$_aM_B - {}_hM_B - {}_fM_B = {}_hX_B + {}_fX_B$$
$$_aM_B - {}_hM_B - {}_hX_A = {}_hX_B + {}_hM_A$$
$$M_3 = X_2.$$

That is, M_3 in Figure 6B is drawn so that its vertical distance from M_2 is equal to the vertical distance from G_2Q_2 of that point on A's X_2 which is the same horizontal distance from G_2G_1 as the given point on B's M_3 is from Q_2Q_1. X_2 in Figure 6B is drawn so that its vertical distance from X_1 is equal to the vertical distance from G_1Q_1 of that point on A's M_1 which is the same horizontal distance from G_2G_1 as the given point on B's X_2 is from Q_2Q_1.

The multiplier, which (for A) is equal to the increment in income divided by the autonomous increment in exports, is derived geometrically as follows:

$$k_A = \frac{G_1K}{G_1G_2} = \frac{1}{\dfrac{LJ}{G_1K} + \dfrac{JK}{G_1K}} = \frac{1}{\dfrac{DJ}{G_2L} + \dfrac{LD}{G_2L} + \dfrac{FK}{G_1K} + \dfrac{JF}{G_1K}}$$

$$= \frac{1}{M'_B - X'_A + M'_A - X'_B}$$

Similarly, for B:

$$k_B = \frac{Q_1 T}{Q_1 Q_2} = \cfrac{1}{\dfrac{VU}{Q_1 T} + \dfrac{UT}{Q_1 T}} = \cfrac{1}{\dfrac{VR}{Q_2 V} + \dfrac{RU}{Q_2 V} + \dfrac{UW}{Q_1 T} + \dfrac{WT}{Q_1 T}}$$

$$= \frac{1}{M'_B - X'_A + M'_A - X'_B}$$

Hence,

(4. 5) $$k_A = k_B = \frac{1}{M'_A - X'_A + M'_B - X'_B}.$$

Again, the multiplier in both sectors is identical, and the increase in A's income is exactly equal to the decrease in B's income.

IV. Inter-Sector Multipliers
(with savings and investment)

Let us now assume that there is saving and investment in both sectors. In this case, $E = C + I + X$ and $Y = C + S + M$, and equilibrium requires that $Z'_A = L'_A = -L'_B = -Z'_B$; that is, excess savings and the external balance must be equal in each economy, and the net foreign lending of the one sector must equal the net foreign borrowing of the other.

We define the intra-expenditure inter-sector multiplier for A as the change in A's income divided by an autonomous change in A's excess savings. This multiplier is found to be [5]

[5] As follows: the equilibrium condition, expressed in terms of induced changes, is that $\Delta Z_B = \Delta L_B$. Hence,

$$Z'_B \Delta Y_B = L'_B \Delta Y_B - L'_A \Delta Y_A$$

giving us

(a) $$\Delta Y_B = -\frac{L'_A}{Z'_B - L'_B} \Delta Y_A.$$

Now A's final increase in income is composed as follows:

$$\Delta Y_A = -{}_a\Delta Z_A + {}_n\Delta C_A + {}_n\Delta I_A + {}_n\Delta X_A - {}_f\Delta X_A + {}_f\Delta M_A$$
$$= -\Delta Z_A + C'_A \Delta Y_A + I'_A \Delta Y_A + X'_A \Delta Y_A - L'_B \Delta Y_B.$$

Then,

(b) $$-\Delta Z_A - L'_B \Delta Y_B = \Delta Y_A (1 - C'_A - I'_A - X'_A) = \Delta Y_A (Z'_A - L'_A).$$

Substituting (a) in (b), we have

$$\Delta Y_A (Z'_A - L'_A) = -\Delta Z_A + \Delta Y_A \left(\frac{L'_A L'_B}{Z'_B - L'_B}\right)$$

which gives us

$$\frac{\Delta Y_A}{-\Delta Z_A} = \frac{Z'_B - L'_B}{Z'_A Z'_B - L'_A Z'_B - Z'_B L'_B} = \frac{1 - \dfrac{L'_B}{Z'_B}}{Z'_A - L'_A - Z'_A \dfrac{L'_B}{Z'_B}}.$$

If I' and X' are zero in both sectors, this is the same as Dr. Machlup's "investment multiplier" (*International Trade and the National Income Multiplier*, pp. 126-128).

$$(4.6) \qquad _Ak_A = \frac{\Delta Y_A}{-\Delta Z_A} = \frac{1 - \dfrac{L'_B}{Z'_B}}{(1 - \dfrac{L'_B}{Z'_B}) Z'_A - L'_A}$$

$$= \frac{1}{Z'_A - L'_A \left(\dfrac{1}{1 - \dfrac{L'_B}{Z'_B}} \right)}$$

Likewise we may define the extra-expenditure inter-sector multiplier for A as the induced change in A's income divided by the autonomous change in B's excess savings. This gives us [6]

$$(4.7) \qquad _Bk_A = \frac{\Delta Y_A}{-\Delta Z_B} = \frac{- \dfrac{L'_B}{Z'_B}}{(1 - \dfrac{L'_B}{Z'_B}) Z'_A - L'_A} .$$

The inter-expenditure inter-sector multiplier may be defined for A as the induced change in A's income divided by the autonomous change in A's external balance. Since an autonomous export from A to B may be regarded as a simultaneous autonomous rise in expenditure in A and an equal autonomous fall in expenditure in B, the inter-expenditure multiplier is simply the difference between the intra-expenditure and extra-expenditure multipliers. We then have by (4.6) and (4.7)

---

[6] As follows: A's change in income consists of the initial increment in the external balance plus the home-induced changes:

$$\Delta Y_A = _f\Delta L_A + _h\Delta C_A + _h\Delta I_A + _h\Delta X_A$$
$$= - L'_B \Delta Y_B + C'_A \Delta Y_A + I'_A \Delta Y_A + X'_A \Delta Y_A$$

so that

(c) $\qquad - L'_B \Delta Y_B = \Delta Y_A (1 - C'_A - I'_A - X'_A) = \Delta Y_A (Z'_A - L'_A).$

Since $\Delta Y_B = _Bk_B(- \Delta Z_B)$, substitution of (4.6) in (c) gives

$$\Delta Y_A (Z'_A - L'_A) = - L'_B \frac{1}{Z'_B - L'_B \left(\dfrac{1}{1 - \dfrac{L'_A}{Z'_A}} \right)} (- \Delta Z_B)$$

from which we derive

$$\frac{Y_A}{- Z_B} = \frac{1}{Z'_A (1 - \dfrac{Z'_B}{L'_B}) + L'_A \dfrac{Z'_B}{L'_B}} = \frac{- \dfrac{L'_B}{Z'_B}}{(1 - \dfrac{L'_B}{Z'_B}) Z'_A - L'_A} .$$

$$(4.8) \qquad _{A-B}k_A = {}_A k_A - {}_B k_A = \cfrac{1}{(1 - \cfrac{L'_B}{Z'_B})Z'_A - L'_A}.$$

This is the generalized form of Dr. Machlup's "export multiplier." [7] Equilibrium is established in both sectors by the intersection of the external balance and excess savings functions, and the net foreign lending (F_1Y) of A is equal to the net

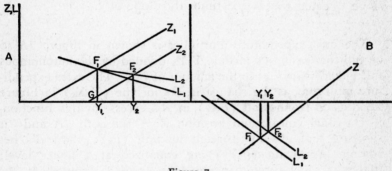

Figure 7.

foreign borrowing (F_1Y) of B. A fall in A's excess savings schedule (that is, a rise in consumption or investment or both) leads to a rise in A's income and a fall in its external balance (by a movement along the home-induced external balance function L_1). The fall in the external balance constitutes a

[7] *International Trade and the National Income Multiplier*, p. 78. The interexpenditure multiplier may be derived directly. The equilibrium condition in terms of induced changes is that $\Delta Z_A = - \Delta Z_B$. That is,

$$(d) \qquad \Delta Y_B = - \frac{Z'_A}{Z'_B} \Delta Y_A.$$

A's final increase in income is made up as follows:

$$(e) \qquad \Delta Y_A = {}_a\Delta L_A + {}_h\Delta C_A + {}_h\Delta I_A + {}_h\Delta X_A - {}_f\Delta X_A + {}_f\Delta M_A$$
$$= \Delta L + C'_A\Delta Y_A + I'_A\Delta Y_A + X'_A\Delta Y_A - L'_B\Delta Y_B.$$

Substituting (d) in (e) we obtain

$$\Delta Y_A = \Delta L_A + C'_A\Delta Y_A + I'_A\Delta Y_A + X'_A\Delta Y_A + L'_B\frac{Z'_A}{Z'_B}\Delta Y_A$$

giving us

$$\Delta L_A = \Delta Y_A(1 - C'_A - I'_A - X'_A - L'_B\frac{Z'_A}{Z'_B}) = \Delta Y_A(Z'_A - L'_A - L'_B\frac{Z'_A}{Z'_B})$$

so that

$$\frac{\Delta Y_A}{\Delta L_A} = \cfrac{1}{Z'_A - L'_A - Z'_A\cfrac{L'_B}{Z'_B}} = \cfrac{1}{(1 - \cfrac{L'_B}{Z'_B})Z'_A - L'_A}.$$

rise in B's external balance, and is shown by a rise in B's external balance function from L_1 to L_2. B's external balance does not rise by the full amount of the vertical distance between L_1 and L_2 in Figure 7B; that is, B's rise in income will lower B's external balance, and give rise to induced increase in A's external balance. The sum of the home-induced and foreign-induced external balance functions in A is given by L_2, whose slope is equal to $\dfrac{1}{1 - \dfrac{L'_B}{Z'_B}}$ times the slope of L_1.

The intra-expenditure multiplier is shown in Figure 7A to be the change in A's income Y_1Y_2 divided by the autonomous fall in excess savings to the amount of F_1G. The extra-expenditure multiplier is the change in B's income (Y_1Y_2) in Figure 7B divided by the fall (F_1G) in A's excess savings function.

The final equilibrium position is F_2 for both 7A and 7B showing that A's net foreign lending (F_2Y_2) and B's net foreign borrowing (F_2Y_2) are equalized at a lower level; that is, B's net foreign indebtedness to A is diminished. A's rise in income is accompanied by a smaller rise in B's income.

If A is the private economy and B is the government, autonomous changes in private expenditure will have a greater or lesser effect on national income (given the marginal propensity to underspend) according to the slope of L_2 in Figure 7A. If the private economy's marginal propensity to import (e. g., the progressiveness of the tax structure) is high, and if its marginal propensity to export (e. g., the flexibility of unemployment insurance payments) is negative and low, the private economy's marginal propensity to bring about a budget deficit (the slope of L_1) will be steeply negative, and fluctuations in income will be lessened. If the goverment is tempted to increase its expenditures when its revenues increase (i. e., if the government's marginal propensity to import is positive), L'_B will be negative, L_2 will lie above L_1, and the advantages of progressive taxes and flexible unemployment insurance payments will be correspondingly offset. If, on the contrary, government revenues do not affect government expenditures $(L'_B = 0)$, L_2 will coincide with L_1; and if the government has a positive marginal propensity to export, so that increases in revenues lead to reductions in expenditures, L_2 will lie below L_1, and income will be further stabilized. Dynamic considerations show, however, that if the external balance curve becomes too steeply negative, the intersection of the external balance and excess saving functions no longer yields stable equilibrium, and income becomes oscillatory.[8] With a given quantity of money, perfect stability by automatic responses to income changes is therefore theoretically impossible; stability

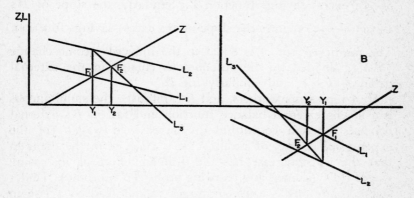

Figure 8.

can then be achieved only by deliberate government expenditure (compensatory shifts of the external balance function) or by means of mechanisms designed to stabilize private expenditure (such as a monetary mechanism effective enough to maintain the excess savings function at the desired position).[9]

The inter-expenditure multiplier may similarly be illustrated graphically (Figure 8). As in Figure 7, equilibrium is set

[8] It is possible, by means of the simple device shown in the appendix to this chapter, to illustrate the dynamics of income changes in the above diagram. The dynamics of income changes will be discussed in Part III. It suffices here to point out that stability requires that the slope of L_2 be greater than Z's slope minus two, i. e., $L'_A \dfrac{1}{1 - \dfrac{L'_B}{Z'_B}} > Z'_A - 2$. If L_2 is steeper than this, income will oscillate explosively, and the automatic mechanisms designed to steepen L_2 will defeat their purpose.

[9] For a detailed discussion of the maintenance of economic stability by means of automatic devices, see Milton Friedman, " A Monetary and Fiscal Framework

where A's net foreign borrowing F_1Y_1 equals B's net foreign lending F_1Y_1. A rise in A's external balance function is at the same time a fall in B's. The fall in B's income will bring about an induced rise in its external balance, constituting an induced fall in A's external balance, which will affect A's income according to A's excess savings function. Hence the slope of L_3 in Figure 8A is equal to $\left(1 - \dfrac{L'_B}{Z'_B}\right)$ times the slope of A's excess savings function Z. Similarly, the slope of B's L_3 is $\left(1 - \dfrac{L'_A}{Z'_A}\right)$ times the slope of B's excess savings function.

The multiplier for A is equal to the induced income change (Y_1Y_2) divided by the autonomous change in the external balance (F_1G), and similarly for B.

If A represents workers, and B capitalists, the simultaneous rise in A's external balance function and fall in B's external balance function constitutes an increase in wages (at the expense, of course, of profits). It is clear from the diagram that the wage-increase has the ultimate effect of increasing wages (A's income) and reducing profits (B's income). Under stable conditions,[10] a rise in wages cannot lead to a rise in profits except by way of shifts in the excess savings and external balance functions.[11]

V. THE GENERALIZED INTER-SECTOR MULTIPLIER

In the previous section we dealt with the inter-sector multiplier when the multiplicand was alternately an autonomous

for Economic Stability," *American Economic Review*, XXXVIII (June, 1948), 245-264. See also the following: Oscar Lange, *Price Flexibility and Employment* (Bloomington, Indiana, 1944); Don Patinkin, "Price Flexibility and Full Employment," *American Economic Review*, XXXVIII (September, 1948), 543-564; A. C. Pigou, "The Classical Stationary State," *Economic Journal*, LIII (December, 1943), 343-351.

[10] If L_3 is too steep (see note 8) income may be oscillatory; i. e., a rise in wages will bring about a rise in profits, followed by a further rise in wages, etc. Thus a temporary rise in profits is theoretically possible.

[11] A retaliatory increase in prices, for instance, would be shown by a downward shift of B's excess savings function. Further induced shifts of the excess saving and external balance functions may be analyzed along the lines of the analysis presented in Lange's *Price Flexibility and Employment*.

change in excess savings and an autonomous change in the external balance. We may now develop a multiplier in which the multiplicand is a change in either excess savings or the external balance, or both. Most changes in expenditure in any system are composed of changes in external as well as internal expenditures. An autonomous investment in a region, for instance, will include payments for imported materials, and payments to capitalists residing in another region; thus the multiplicand consists of a combined fall in excess savings and in the external balance.

Let ΔE be an increment in A's expenditure of which a proportion α is spent in A, and a proportion β is spent in B. Then by (4.6) we have

$$(4.9) \qquad {}_A k_A = \frac{\Delta Y_A}{\alpha \Delta E} = \alpha \; \frac{1 - \dfrac{L'_B}{Z'_B}}{(1 - \dfrac{L'_B}{Z'_B}) Z'_A - L'_A}$$

and by (4.7) we have

$$(4.10) \qquad {}_B k_A = \frac{\Delta Y_A}{\beta \Delta E} = \beta \; \frac{-\dfrac{L'_B}{Z'_B}}{(1 - \dfrac{L'_B}{Z'_B}) Z'_A - L'_A} .$$

Hence, addition of (4.9) and (4.10) gives us

$$(4.11) \qquad {}_{A+B} k_A = \frac{\alpha - (\alpha + \beta) \dfrac{L'_B}{Z'_B}}{(1 - \dfrac{L'_B}{Z'_B}) Z'_A - L'_A} .$$

This may be called the generalized inter-sector multiplier.

If $\alpha = 1$ and $\beta = -1$, (4.11) reduces to (4.8). If $\alpha + \beta = 1$, (4.11) becomes

$$(4.12) \qquad {}_{A+B} k_A = \frac{\alpha - \dfrac{L'_B}{Z'_B}}{(1 - \dfrac{L'_B}{Z'_B}) Z'_A - L'_A} .$$

Thus if $\alpha = 1$, (4.12) is the intra-expenditure multiplier (4.6), and if $\alpha = 0$, (4.12) is the extra-expenditure multiplier (4.7). Machlup's multipliers are clearly all special cases of (4.11).

Let A be an "advanced" region and B a "backward" region. Let us assume that, owing to its maturity, region A has a higher marginal propensity to underspend than region B; and that, because of its self-sufficiency, A's marginal propensity to have a positive external balance is greater than B's. The following values may be assigned to the propensities: $Z'_A = .25$; $L'_A = -.2$; $Z'_B = .19$; and $L'_B = -.4$. Let there be a public expenditure in B, of which $82\frac{1}{2}$ per cent is on-site expenditure, and $17\frac{1}{2}$ per cent goes into imported materials and profits accruing directly to A; then $\beta = .825$ and $\alpha = .175$. Substitution of these values into (4.12) shows that $_{A+B}k_A = 2.275$ and $_{B+A}k_B = 2.275$, that is, that A's income rises equally with B's. Hence over $82\frac{1}{2}$ per cent of the expenditure must accrue directly to the backward region if A is not to benefit more than B.

VI. THE GENERALIZED INTRA-SECTOR MULTIPLIER

In some cases it is desirable to consider the effect of expenditure in a bi-sector economy on the economy as a whole. If an economy consists of two sectors A and B whose marginal propensities to underspend differ, the national income will be affected differently according as expenditure is confined more to one region than to another.

The change in A's income brought about by an increase in expenditure in A and B is given by (4.11); the change in B's income brought about by the same expenditure is given by the symmetrical counterpart of (4.11) (the A and B subscripts interchanged). Hence the change in total income is given by the sum of these two changes, so that

$$(4.13) \quad {}_{A+B}k_{A+B} = \frac{\alpha - (\alpha + \beta)\dfrac{L'_B}{Z'_B}}{(1 - \dfrac{L'_B}{Z'_B})Z'_A - L'_A} + \frac{\beta - (\beta + \alpha)\dfrac{L'_A}{Z'_A}}{(1 - \dfrac{L'_A}{Z'_A})Z'_B - L'_B}$$

which reduces to the form

$$(4.14) \quad {}_{A+B}k_{A+B} = \frac{\alpha Z'_B + \beta Z'_A - (\alpha + \beta)(L'_A + L'_B)}{Z'_A Z'_B - Z'_A L'_B - L'_A Z'_B}.$$

This may be called the generalized intra-sector multiplier.

If $\alpha = -1$ and $\beta = 1$, (4.14) becomes the inter-expenditure intra-sector multiplier, and indicates the increment in income which results from a shift in income from one part of the economy to the other. If $Z'_B = Z'_A$, (4.14) then reduces to zero.

If $a + \beta = 1$, we have the general expression for the multiplier in a bi-sector economy. If $Z'_B = Z'_A$, (4.14) in this case reduces to (4.2). If $Z'_B > Z'_A$, the multiplier will be maximized when the coefficient of the larger (a) is maximized, and conversely. Hence we may infer that public expenditure in a bi-sector economy will generate a maximum increase in national income if it is all concentrated in that region which has the lowest marginal propensity to underspend (which we may expect to be the most backward region). Similarly, assuming that workers' marginal propensity to underspend is higher than capitalists', public expenditure is most effective if the on-site expenditure accrues in its entirety (or as much as possible) to workers.

In a federal system with two provinces or states, each with its own government and tax structure, it is necessary to add to the excess savings function of each province or state a forced excess savings function consisting of taxes less government expenditures (including both federal and provincial taxes and expenditures). Denoting taxes by T, government expenditures by G, and the aggregate (federal plus provincial) deficit in each province by J, we have $J = G - T$. Then, by (4.6)

$$(4.15) \qquad U' = J'(\frac{1}{1 - P'})$$

where U' is defined as the province's marginal propensity to have an aggregate (federal plus provincial) budget deficit within the province, and P' is the government's (federal plus provincial) marginal propensity to spend in that province.[12] We may then deduct U' from Z' for each province in order to obtain the province's marginal propensity to have internal leakages. If taxes are thought of as savings, and government

---

[12] (4.15) is equivalent to the expression $L'_A(\dfrac{1}{1 - \dfrac{L'_B}{Z'_B}})$ in (4.6) and is equal to the slope of L_a in Figure 7A.

expenditures as investment, the expression $Z' - U'$ represents the marginal propensity to underspend in the broad sense. This gives us

$$(4.16) \quad _{A+B}k_{A+B} = \frac{a(Z'_B - U'_B) + \beta(Z'_A - U'_A) - (a + \beta)(L'_A + L'_B)}{(Z'_A - U'_A)(Z'_B - U'_B) - (Z'_A - U'_A)L'_B - (Z'_B - U'_B)L'_A}.$$

Further refinements can be made to such formulas, especially by the use of tri-sector and multi-sector multipliers, in order to achieve any amount of generality desired.

APPENDIX TO CHAPTER 4

A Geometric Presentation of the Dynamic Multiplier

In view of the great controversy that followed the publication of Keynes' *General Theory* about statics and dynamics

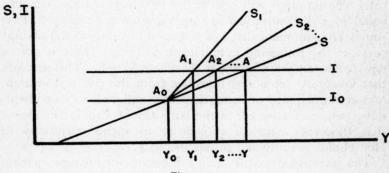

Figure 9.

and about *ex post* and *ex ante* savings and investment, the following diagrammatic exposition of the relationship between the static and dynamic multiplier may be found helpful.

Let us consider a closed economy in which the marginal propensity to invest is zero. In Figure 9, income is measured on the horizontal axis, and savings and investment on the vertical axis. The initial equilibrium is determined at the point of intersection, A_0, of the savings and investment curves S and I_0. These curves represent the amounts which individuals and firms will wish to save and invest at given incomes. It is assumed that the instantaneous effect of an autonomous rise in investment is to raise income by the amount of the rise in investment. The new income is not spent immediately; consequently the "instantaneous marginal propensity to save" is equal to unity.

A rise in the investment schedule to I has the effect of raising income by the same amount; hence, the slope of the instantaneous savings curve S_1 is equal to unity, and a temporary equilibrium is established at A_1. At A_1, actual (*ex post*) savings and investment are equal, but planned (*ex ante*) savings and investment (as shown by the points of the S and I curves at the level of income Y_1) are unequal. Since planned investment exceeds planned savings, income must rise. The amount by which it must rise in the next period is determined by the amount by which it has already risen (Y_0Y_1); specifically, consumption will rise in the next period by an amount equal to Y_0Y_1 multiplied by the marginal propensity to consume. Diagrammatically, this is shown by a fall in the savings curve in the following period from S_1 to S_2. There is now a new temporary equilibrium at A_2, where $S_2 = I$. (This assumes that inventory depletions resulting from the rise in consumption are anticipated or instantaneously replaced, so that investment remains unaltered; in the language of Part I, this means that Business' marginal propensity to spend eventually to Households is unity and instantaneous.)

The savings curve will again fall because of the new increase of income from Y_1 to Y_2. And so the process will continue until the actual savings curve has finally coincided (after an infinite lapse of time) with the scheduled savings curve S.

From one point of view—*ex ante*—savings and investment are equal only in complete equilibrium (at the points A_0 and A); from another—*ex post*—they are always equal (at the "temporary equilibrium" points $A_1, A_2, \cdots$). If we wish to regard savings and investment as being always equal, we must define them in such a way that the marginal propensity to save keeps changing as income moves from one point of equilibrium to another; in this case we have a "moving equilibrium" over time.

If the assumption that inventory depletions are instantaneously replaced is relaxed, there will also be temporary investment curves, negative in slope, one of which will finally coincide with the scheduled investment curve. It is possible also to construct a geometric treatment of this process when there exists a marginal propensity to invest. This geometric analysis may be adapted to various different assumptions, and may readily be extended to the bi-sectoral case.

CHAPTER 5

ALTERNATIVE FORMULATIONS OF THE MULTIPLIER FOR TWO SECTORS

I. FORMULATION IN TERMS OF MARGINAL PROPENSITIES TO SPEND

The formulas developed in the previous chapter may also be presented in an alternative and, for many purposes, a more convenient form.

Let there be two sectors, 1 and 2, whose receipts are respectively Y_1 and Y_2. Each of these sector's receipts shall be assumed to consist of (1) autonomous disbursements, (2) induced internal disbursements, and (3) induced external disbursements (disbursements to that sector by the other sector). Induced disbursement is (following the terminology of Dr. Machlup) that disbursement which is brought about by changes in receipts. A sector's induced internal disbursement is therefore equal to the change in that sector's receipts multiplied by its marginal propensity to spend internally (to use Dr. Lange's phrase) or marginal propensity to "intraspend"; and induced external disbursement is equal to the change in the other sector's receipts multiplied by *its* marginal propensity to spend to the given sector, that is, its marginal propensity to spend externally (in the Lange terminology) or marginal propensity to "extraspend." Denoting autonomous changes in disbursements to sectors 1 and 2 by dE_1 and dE_2 respectively, sector 1's marginal propensities to intraspend and extraspend by $_1E'_1$ and $_1E'_2$, respectively, and sector 2's marginal propensities to intraspend and extraspend by $_2E'_2$ and $_2E'_1$, respectively, we may represent the changes in the two sectors' receipts by the following two equilibrium equations:

(5.1)
$$\begin{cases} dY_1 = dE_1 + {}_1E'_1 dY_1 + {}_2E'_1 dY_2 \\ dY_2 = dE_2 + {}_1E'_2 dY_1 + {}_2E'_2 dY_2. \end{cases}$$

Now we may consider the effect of any disturbance in disbursements on the receipts of both sectors. Such a disturbance, as we saw in the last chapter, will in the general case consist of a disturbance in disbursements in both sectors, either in the form of a change in disbursements in the same direction in both sectors, or an autonomous transfer of disbursements from one sector to another. Let this autonomous disturbance be represented by the symbol dA. We may then make the following definitions:

$$(5.2) \qquad e_1 = \frac{dE_1}{dA} \qquad e_2 = \frac{dE_2}{dA}.$$

The symbols e_1 and e_2 are equivalent to the α and β of the last chapter; that is, e_1 represents the proportion of the autonomous disbursement in sector 1 to the total autonomous disturbance, and similarly for e_2. If, therefore, the autonomous disturbance consists of an autonomous change of disbursements in the same direction in both sectors, dA is considered to be the total change in disbursements (the sum of dE_1 and dE_2), and e_1 and e_2 are simply the proportions of this autonomous disbursement which are made in sectors 1 and 2. If, on the other hand, the autonomous disturbance consists of an autonomous transfer of disbursements from one sector to another (say from 1 to 2), dA is considered to be the amount of this autonomous transfer, and $e = 1$ while $e_2 = -1$.

We may also define the multiplier for each sector as the ratio of the increment in its receipts resulting from the disturbance, to the disturbance. Representing the multipliers for sectors 1 and 2 by k_1 and k_2, we may express this definition by the equations:

$$(5.3) \qquad k_1 = \frac{dY_1}{dA} \qquad k_2 = \frac{dY_2}{dA}.$$

Now we may collect the common terms in the system of equations (5.1) and rewrite it as follows:

$$(5.4) \qquad \begin{cases} (1 - {}_1E'_1)\,dY_1 - {}_2E'_1\,dY_2 = dE_1 \\ - {}_1E'_2\,dY_1 + (1 - {}_2E'_2)\,dY_2 = dE_2. \end{cases}$$

Dividing the system of equations (5.4) through by the differential element dA, we obtain, after substitution of (5.2) and (5.3), the following system of equations:

(5.5)
$$\begin{cases} (1 - {}_1E'_1)k_1 - {}_2E'_1k_2 = e_1 \\ - {}_1E'_2k_1 + (1 - {}_2E'_2)k_2 = e_2. \end{cases}$$

In order to evaluate the multipliers k_1 and k_2, we solve equation (5.5). The solution, expressed in determinants, is as follows:

(5.6)
$$k_1 = \dfrac{\begin{vmatrix} e_1 & - {}_2E'_1 \\ e_2 & 1 - {}_2E'_2 \end{vmatrix}}{\begin{vmatrix} 1 - {}_1E'_1 & - {}_2E'_1 \\ - {}_1E'_2 & 1 - {}_2E'_2 \end{vmatrix}}$$

$$k_2 = \dfrac{\begin{vmatrix} 1 - {}_1E'_1 & e_1 \\ - {}_1E'_2 & e_2 \end{vmatrix}}{\begin{vmatrix} 1 - {}_1E'_1 & - {}_2E'_1 \\ - {}_1E'_2 & 1 - {}_2E'_2 \end{vmatrix}} .$$

Written out, these solutions are:

(5.7)
$$k_1 = \frac{e_1(1 - {}_2E'_2) + e_2({}_2E'_1)}{(1 - {}_1E'_1)(1 - {}_2E'_2) - {}_1E'_2 \cdot {}_2E'_1}$$

$$k_2 = \frac{e_2(1 - {}_1E'_1) + e_1({}_1E'_2)}{(1 - {}_1E'_1)(1 - {}_2E'_2) - {}_1E'_2 \cdot {}_2E'_1}$$

The multiplier formulas developed by Dr. Metzler in 1942 may be considered as special cases of the above equations (5.7).[1]

II. Formulation in Terms of Marginal Propensities to Spend Eventually

The formulas presented by Dr. Lange[2] may similarly be shown to be equivalent to our equations (5.7). Dividing the numerator and denominator of the first equation in (5.7) by the term $(1 - {}_2E'_2)$, and the numerator and denominator of the second by $(1 - {}_1E'_1)$, we obtain:

---

[1] Metzler, "Underemployment Equilibrium in International Trade." His successive multiplier formulas hold for the cases in which (1) $e_1 = 1$ and $e_2 = 0$ (his equation (9) and (10)), (2) $e_1 = -1$ and $e_2 = 1$ (his equations (11)), and (3) $e_1 = 0$ and $e_2 = 1$ (his equations (12)).

[2] Lange, "The Theory of the Multiplier."

(5. 8)

$$k_1 = \frac{e_2 + e_1 \dfrac{{}_2E'_1}{1 - {}_2E'_2}}{1 - {}_1E'_1 - {}_1E'_2 \dfrac{{}_2E'_1}{1 - {}_2E'_2}}$$

$$k_2 = \frac{e_2 + e_1 \dfrac{{}_1E'_2}{1 - {}_1E'_1}}{1 - {}_2E'_2 - {}_2E'_1 \dfrac{{}_1E'_2}{1 - {}_1E'_1}} \; .$$

The fractions appearing in numerator and denominator of both these formulas may be recognized as being equivalent to Lange's concept of the "other systems' *marginal propensity to spend back*,"[3] which he denotes by the symbol R'. We may therefore define sector 2's marginal propensity to spend back to sector 1, and sector 1's marginal propensity to spend back to sector 2, respectively, as follows:

(5. 9)
$$\qquad {}_2R'_1 = \frac{{}_2E'_1}{1 - {}_2E'_2} \qquad\qquad {}_1R'_2 = \frac{{}_1E'_2}{1 - {}_1E'_1}$$

so that equations (5.8) become

(5. 10)

$$k_1 = \frac{e_1 + {}_2R'_1 e_2}{1 - ({}_1E'_1 + {}_2R'_1 \cdot {}_1E'_2)}$$

$$k_2 = \frac{e_2 + {}_1R'_2 e_1}{1 - ({}_2E'_2 + {}_1R'_2 \cdot {}_2E'_1)} \; .$$

The Lange formulas are all special cases of the first equation in (5. 10).[4]

[3] "The Theory of the Multiplier," p. 233. Since, however (as we saw in Chapter 2), Lange assumes in his dynamic formulation that the spending back occurs instantaneously, his "other systems' *marginal propensity to spend back*" to the given system is equivalent to the other systems' marginal propensity to *spend* to the given system. In other words, the other sector has a zero marginal propensity to spend internally, and its marginal propensity to spend back is equivalent to its marginal propensity to spend externally.

[4] Lange's "internal spending multiplier" (p. 233) is the case in which $e_1 = 1$ and $e_2 = 0$. His "total spending multiplier" (pp. 234-235) is the case in which $e_1 = {}_1E'_1$ and $e_2 = {}_1E'_2$; that is, the case in which autonomous disbursement is distributed between sectors in the same proportion as is the given sector's marginal propensity to spend. The first case would illustrate the situation in which the autonomous disturbance is an increase in government expenditure in country 1, and the second the situation in which it is a fall in taxes in country 1.

The concept of an "international reflection ratio," recently formulated by Dr. Polak,[5] is identical to Lange's "marginal propensity to spend back." It is defined as "the ratio between the increase in a country's imports (as effect) and the increase in its exports (as cause)."[6] Denoting sector 1's spending to sector 2 (its imports from sector 2) by $_1E_2$ (or, alternatively, M_1) and sector 2's spending to sector 1 (sector 1's exports to sector 2) by $_2E_1$ (or X_1), we have:

$$(5.11) \qquad _1R'_2 = \frac{d_1E_2/dY_1}{1 - d_1E_1/dY_1} = \frac{d_1E_2}{dY_1 - d_1E_1} = \frac{d_1E_2}{d_2E_1} = \frac{dM_1}{dX_1} .$$

It follows that we may set up a system of equations in terms of "exports" and "marginal propensities to spend eventually" as well as a system in terms of "receipts" and "marginal propensities to spend." We may thus express the change in each sector's exports (which is the change in the other sector's imports) as a function of the other sector's change in exports. Let dF_1 and dF_2 be autonomous changes in exports in sectors 1 and 2. Then we may write the equations[7]

$$(5.12) \qquad \begin{cases} dX_1 = dF_1 + 0dX_1 + _2R'_1dX_2 \\ dX_2 = dF_2 + _1R'_2dX_1 + 0dX_2. \end{cases}$$

The system of equations (5.12) is equivalent to the system of equations (5.1).

Let dB be a disturbance in exports. Then, as in (5.2), we may define

$$(5.13) \qquad f_1 = \frac{dF_1}{dB} \qquad\qquad f_2 = \frac{dF_2}{dB} .$$

We may also define the "multipliers" (the ratio of a sector's change in exports to the autonomous disturbance) for this kind of system, for the two sectors, as follows:

$$(5.14) \qquad l_1 = \frac{dX_1}{dB} \qquad\qquad l_2 = \frac{dX_2}{dB} .$$

---

[5] J. J. Polak, "An International Economic System" (abstract), *Econometrica*, Vol. 18, No. 1 (January, 1950), pp. 70-72.

[6] *Ibid.*, p. 71.

[7] The zero coefficients are inserted for the sake of symmetry.

Rearranging the terms of equations (5.12) we obtain

(5.15)
$$\begin{cases} dX_1 - {}_2R'_1 dX_2 = dF_1 \\ - {}_1R'_2 dX_1 + dX_2 = dF_2. \end{cases}$$

Dividing equations (5.15) through by dB, and solving, we obtain the "multipliers":

(5.16)

$$l_1 = \frac{\begin{vmatrix} f_1 & -{}_2R'_1 \\ f_2 & 1 \end{vmatrix}}{\begin{vmatrix} 1 & -{}_2R'_1 \\ -{}_1R'_2 & 1 \end{vmatrix}}$$

$$l_2 = \frac{\begin{vmatrix} 1 & f_1 \\ -{}_1R'_2 & f_2 \end{vmatrix}}{\begin{vmatrix} 1 & -{}_2R'_1 \\ -{}_1R'_2 & 1 \end{vmatrix}}$$

which, in expanded form, may be written

(5.17) $$l_1 = \frac{f_1 + {}_2R'_1 f_2}{1 - {}_1R'_2 \cdot {}_2R'_1} \qquad l_2 = \frac{f_2 + {}_1R'_2 f_1}{1 - {}_1R'_2 \cdot {}_2R'_1}.$$

These are "multipliers" in the sense that each sector's *external receipts* only are considered as "income." Internal receipts and disbursements are implicitly present in the equations, since the external receipts and disbursements are derived from them; but they are not dealt with explicitly. The sectors are considered as being vertically integrated, so that internal transactions do not enter explicitly into the system. We may call the above multipliers "external receipts multipliers" as opposed to "total receipts multipliers." [8]

The "external receipts" and "total receipts" multipliers are related in a precise way. The denominators of (5.16) and (5.17) may be written (by substitution of (5.9)):

(5.18) $$1 - {}_1R'_2 \cdot {}_2R'_1 = 1 - \frac{{}_1E'_2 \cdot {}_2E'_1}{(1 - {}_1E'_1)(1 - {}_2E'_2)}$$
$$= \frac{(1 - {}_1E'_1)(1 - {}_2E'_2) - {}_1E'_2 \cdot {}_2E'_1}{(1 - {}_1E'_1)(1 - {}_2E'_2)}$$

---

[8] External receipts multipliers are useful for certain international trade problems in which currency inconvertibility requires a country's imports from another to be a function of its exports to that country alone. This was pointed out to me by Dr. Donald B. Marsh.

Comparing (5.18) and (5.17) with (5.7) we find that (5.19)

$$l_1 = \frac{\{f_1 + {}_2R'_1 f_2\}\{(1 - {}_1E'_1)(1 - {}_2E'_2)\}}{(1 - {}_1E'_1)(1 - {}_2E'_2) - {}_1E'_2 \cdot {}_2E'_1}$$

$$= (1 - {}_1E'_1)\frac{f_1 + {}_2R'_1 f_2}{e_1 + {}_2R'_1 e_2} k_1$$

$$l_2 = \frac{\{f_2 + {}_1R'_2 f_1\}\{(1 - {}_1E'_1)(1 - {}_2E'_2)\}}{(1 - {}_1E'_1)(1 - {}_2E'_2) - {}_1E'_2 \cdot {}_2E'_1}$$

$$= (1 - {}_2E'_2)\frac{f_2 + {}_1R'_2 f_1}{e_2 + {}_1R'_2 e_1} k_2.$$

The effect of a disturbance on sector 1's export surplus is given by the difference between these two multipliers, that is to say, by $l_1 - l_2$.[9]

III. COMPARISON OF THESE FORMULATIONS WITH THAT OF THE PREVIOUS CHAPTER

The formulations of the above sections may readily be translated into the notation of the last chapter, and hence compared with Professor Machlup's formulation of the multiplier.

The marginal propensity of sector A to spend to sector B is equal to its marginal propensity to import from B less its marginal propensity (if any) to export to B. In the terminology of the last chapter this is equal to minus the marginal propensity of that sector to have a positive external balance. Interchanging the subscripts 1 and 2 with the subscripts A and B respectively, we have the equivalence:

$$(5.20) \qquad {}_1E'_2 = {}_AE'_B = -L'_A \qquad {}_2E'_1 = {}_BE'_A = -L'_B.$$

Similarly, that part of a sector's income that is not spent internally consists of (1) its external spending and (2) its excess savings. Hence we may establish the further equivalence:

---

[9] In the case in which $f_1 = 1$ and $f_2 = 0$ (an autonomous export from 1 to 2) we have

$$l_1 - l_2 = \frac{(1 - {}_1E'_1 - {}_1E'_2)(1 - {}_2E'_2)}{(1 - {}_1E'_1)(1 - {}_2E'_2) - {}_1E'_2 \cdot {}_2E'_1}$$

which is the same as a formula given by Metzler ("Underemployment Equilibrium in International Trade," the third equation of (13)).

(5. 21)

$$1 - {}_1E'_1 = 1 - {}_AE'_A = -L'_A + Z'_A$$

$$1 - {}_2E'_2 = 1 - {}_BE'_B = -L'_B + Z'_B.$$

Substituting (5.20) and (5.21) in (5.9), we obtain the equivalences:

(5. 22)

$$_1R'_2 = {}_AR'_B = \cfrac{1}{1 - \cfrac{Z'_A}{L'_A}}$$

$$_2R'_1 = {}_BR'_A = \cfrac{1}{1 - \cfrac{Z'_B}{L'_B}}\ .$$

Since e_1 and e_2 are equivalent to the α and β of the previous chapter, equations (5.8) become

(5.23)

$$k_A = \frac{a + \beta_B R'_A}{Z'_A - L'_A(1 - {}_BR'_A)} = \cfrac{a\left(1 - \cfrac{L'_B}{Z'_B}\right) - \beta\,\cfrac{L'_B}{Z'_B}}{\left(1 - \cfrac{L'_B}{Z'_B}\right)Z'_A - L'_A}$$

$$k_B = \frac{\beta + a_A R'_B}{Z'_B - L'_B(1 - {}_AR'_B)} = \cfrac{\beta\left(1 - \cfrac{L'_A}{Z'_A}\right) - a\,\cfrac{L'_A}{Z'_A}}{\left(1 - \cfrac{L'_A}{Z'_A}\right)Z'_B - L'_B}\ .$$

These formulas are equivalent to equation (4.11) of the previous chapter.

PART III

SEVERAL SECTORS

CHAPTER 6

THE MULTI-SECTOR MULTIPLIER

I. FORMULATION OF THE MULTIPLIER

1. We now come to the mathematical formulation of the multiplier in a multi-sector economy. The economy is divided into n sectors, $1, 2, \cdots, n$. The receipts per unit of time of the i-th sector of the economy may be denoted by Y_i, and the disbursements per unit of time of the j-th sector of the economy to the i-th sector of the economy may be denoted by $_jE_i$. Corresponding to any sector of the economy, say the j-th, there is an array of its disbursements to every sector of the economy, which may be denoted by the column vector

$$(6.1) \qquad _jE = \begin{bmatrix} _jE_1 \\ _jE_2 \\ \cdot \\ \cdot \\ _jE_n \end{bmatrix}.$$

The disbursement function of sector j is the functional relationship between this array or vector of disbursements, at time t, to its receipts—Y_j—at time $t-1$. This disbursement function may be written (ignoring the time-subscripts for simplicity of notation):

$$(6.2) \qquad _jE(Y_j) = \begin{bmatrix} _jE_1 \\ _jE_2 \\ \cdot \\ \cdot \\ _jE_n \end{bmatrix} (Y_j).$$

The derivative of the disbursement function is the vector of j's marginal propensities to spend, written

$$(6.3) \qquad _jE'(Y_j) = \begin{bmatrix} _jE'_1 \\ _jE'_2 \\ \cdot \\ \cdot \\ _jE'_n \end{bmatrix}$$

where $_jE'_i = \dfrac{\partial_j E_i}{\partial Y_j}$ is j's marginal propensity to spend to i. The array of all sector's vectors of marginal propensities to spend, arranged in a row, is the matrix of marginal propensities to spend, or the multiplier matrix:

$$(6.4) \qquad M = \begin{bmatrix} _1E'_1 & _2E'_1 & \cdots & _nE'_1 \\ _1E'_2 & _2E'_2 & \cdots & _nE'_2 \\ \cdot & \cdot & \cdot & \cdot \\ _1E'_n & _2E'_n & \cdots & _nE'_n \end{bmatrix}.$$

2. The receipts of the i-th sector of the economy consist of (1) an autonomous factor (not induced by any sector's receipts), (2) internally-induced disbursement, and (3) externally-induced disbursements. A change in sector i's receipts may be brought about by an autonomous change in disbursements to [1] sector i, or by changes in disbursements to sector i which are brought about by changes in any sector's receipts. Since by hypothesis disbursements follow receipts by one lag, the change in a sector's receipts at time t is equal to the autonomous change in disbursements to that sector at time t, plus the induced changes in disbursements to that sector at time t, that is, plus the change in all sectors' receipts at time $t-1$, multiplied by their respective marginal propensities to spend to sector i. This may be stated in the form of an equation:

$$(6.5) \quad dY_i(t) = dE_i + \sum_{j=1}^{n} {}_jE_i'dY_j(t-1) \qquad (i = 1, 2, \cdots, n)$$

where dE_i is the change in disbursement to i at time t and $dY_j(t)$ is the autonomous receipts of sector j at time t.

From (6.5) we obtain the system of difference equations which describe the multi-sector economy:

$$(6.6)$$

$$\begin{cases} dY_1(t) = dE_1 + {}_1E'_1dY_1(t-1) + {}_2E'_1dY_2(t-1) + \cdots + {}_nE'_1dY_n(t- \\ dY_2(t) = dE_2 + {}_1E'_2dY_1(t-1) + {}_2E'_2dY_2(t-1) + \cdots + {}_nE'_2dY_n(t- \\ \cdot \quad \cdot \quad \cdot \quad \cdot \quad \cdot \quad \cdot \quad \cdot \quad \cdot \quad \cdot \quad \cdot \quad \cdot \quad \cdot \quad \cdot \quad \cdot \quad \cdot \\ dY_n(t) = dE_n + {}_1E'_ndY_1(t-1) + {}_2E'_ndY_2(t-1) + \cdots + {}_nE'_ndY_n(t- \end{cases}$$

[1] The word "to" is used here, rather than "in," at the suggestion of Dr. Machlup, in order to avoid a possible ambiguity. The word "to" should be understood to include disbursements to sector i by sector i.

This system of equations may be written in matric form:

$$(6.7)\quad \begin{bmatrix} dY_1(t) \\ dY_2(t) \\ \cdot \\ dY_n(t) \end{bmatrix} = \begin{bmatrix} dE_1 \\ dE_2 \\ \cdot \\ dE_n \end{bmatrix} + \begin{bmatrix} {}_1E'_1 & {}_2E'_1 & \cdots & {}_nE'_1 \\ {}_1E'_2 & {}_2E'_2 & \cdots & {}_nE'_2 \\ \cdot & \cdot & \cdots & \cdot \\ {}_1E'_n & {}_2E'_n & \cdots & {}_nE'_n \end{bmatrix} \begin{bmatrix} dY_1(t-1) \\ dY_2(t-1) \\ \cdot \\ dY_n(t-1) \end{bmatrix}$$

or more concisely,

$$(6.8)\qquad dY(t) = dE + M\, dY(t-1).$$

3. The concept of the multi-sector multiplier must now be defined. It may be defined in scalar form as the resulting change in sector i's receipts after a specified lapse of time (including an infinite lapse of time as a special case[2]), divided by the autonomous disturbance in disbursements. Two kinds of disturbance may be distinguished: (1) an autonomous net change in disbursements throughout the economy— $\sum_{i=1}^{n} dE_i$, and (2) an autonomous transfer of disbursements, such as an import, from one sector or group of sectors of the economy to another— ΣdE_i, where the sum now runs over only those values of i for which $dE_i > 0$. If $\sum_{i=1}^{n} dE_i \neq 0$, so that there is a net change in total disbursements, the first definition may be used; if $\sum_{i=1}^{n} dE_i = 0$, that is, if there is no net change in disbursements, but only a shift in disbursements among sectors, then the second should be used. In both cases the autonomous disturbance may be denoted by dA.

The proportion of the autonomous disbursement which is made to sector i may be denoted by e_i. The multiplier for sector i, denoted by k_i, is the proportion of i's change in receipts to the autonomous disturbance. Hence we have the two definitions

$$(6.9)\qquad k_i = \frac{dY_i}{dA} \qquad\qquad e_i = \frac{dE_i}{dA}.$$

---

[2] This special case corresponds, under stable conditions, to the original definition of the multiplier. The multiplier for a finite period of time (developed by Kahn, Clark, Bretherton, Burchardt and Rutherford, and Machlup) has been called by Professor Samuelson the "truncated multiplier"; see "A Fundamental Multiplier Identity," also Lange, "The Theory of the Multiplier."

Substituting (6.9) in (6.6) we obtain the equivalent system of equations

(6. 10)

$$\begin{cases} k_1(t) = e_1 + {}_1E'_1k_1(t-1) + {}_2E'_1k_2(t-1) + \cdots + {}_nE'_1k_n(t-1) \\ k_2(t) = e_2 + {}_1E'_2k_1(t-1) + {}_2E'_2k_2(t-1) + \cdots + {}_nE'_2k_n(t-1) \\ \cdot \cdot \cdot \cdot \cdot \cdot \cdot \\ k_n(t) = e_n + {}_1E'_nk_1(t-1) + {}_2E'_nk_2(t-1) + \cdots + {}_nE'_nk_n(t-1) \end{cases}$$

which again may be written in the matric form

(6. 11)
$$\begin{bmatrix} k_1(t) \\ k_2(t) \\ \cdot \\ k_n(t) \end{bmatrix} = \begin{bmatrix} e_1 \\ e_2 \\ \cdot \\ e_n \end{bmatrix} + \begin{bmatrix} {}_1E'_1 & {}_2E'_1 \cdots {}_nE'_1 \\ {}_1E'_2 & {}_2E'_2 \cdots {}_nE'_2 \\ \cdot & \cdot \cdots \cdot \\ {}_1E'_n & {}_2E'_n \cdots {}_nE'_n \end{bmatrix} \begin{bmatrix} k_1(t-1) \\ k_2(t-1) \\ \cdot \cdot \cdot \\ k_n(t-1) \end{bmatrix}$$

or in abbreviated form

(6. 12) $$k(t) = e + Mk(t-1).$$

These two forms, represented by equations (6.6), (6.7), and (6.8) on the one hand, and by (6.10), (6.11) and (6.12) on the other, are entirely interchangeable.

II. SOLUTION OF THE MULTIPLIER

1. We shall now derive the matric solution to the multi-sector multiplier, and proceed in the later sections of this chapter with the scalar solution.

We start, in the analysis, from a premise of initial equilibrium; that is, we assume that in the initial time-period ($t = 0$) the flows of receipts are unchanging and in a position of equilibrium. Hence the change in receipts at time 0 is nil. The initial condition of the system is, therefore:

(6. 13) $$dY(0) = 0 \qquad\qquad k(0) = 0.$$

Substituting this initial condition in (6.8) and (6.12), we find that in the period $t = 1$ the receipts and multiplier vectors become

(6. 14) $$dY(1) = dE \qquad\qquad k(1) = e.$$

Continuing with this process we find that [3]

$$dY(2) = dE + MdE = [I + M]dE$$
$$dY(3) = dE + M[I + M]dE = [I + M + M^2]dE$$

(6. 15)

$$. . . . .$$

$$dY(t) = [I + M + M^2 + \cdots + M^{t-1}]dE$$

and similarly that

(6. 16) $$k(t) = [I + M + M^2 + \cdots + M^{t-1}]e.$$

This is the sum of a geometric series which may be written in the form

(6. 17)

$$dY(t) = (I - M^t)(I - M)^{-1}dE$$

$$k(t) = (I - M^t)(I - M)^{-1}e.$$

This series will be convergent (i. e., M^t will approach the zero matrix as t becomes large) if and only if the latent roots of M lie within the unit circle of the complex plane.[4] If this is so, the receipts and multiplier vectors will converge to the ultimate values

(6. 18)

$$\lim_{t \to \infty} dY(t) = (I - M)^{-1}dE$$

$$\lim_{t \to \infty} k(t) = (I - M)^{-1}e.$$

It will be noticed that the solution (6. 17) falls into two parts:

(6. 19)

$$dY(t) = [(I - M)^{-1} - M^t(1 - M)^{-1}]dE$$

$$k(t) = [(I - M)^{-1} - M^t(1 - M)^{-1}]e$$

one of which is independent of time, and the other of which is a function of time. These may be called the stationary and transient parts of the solution. Symbolically this may be represented by the form

---

[3] The following development is found in Samuelson, " A Fundamental Multiplier Identity," p. 224, and in Goodwin, " The Multiplier as Matrix," p. 546.

[4] The conditions that the roots lie within the unit circle are discussed in the following chapter.

(6. 20) $$dY(t) = \overline{dY} + d\hat{Y}(t)$$
$$k(t) = \bar{k} + \hat{k}(t),$$

where the bar indicates the equilibrium value of the receipts or multiplier vector, and the carat denotes the time-path towards that equilibrium. The equilibrium condition is

(6. 21) $$dY(t) = dY(t-1) = \overline{dY}$$
$$k(t) = k(t-1) = \bar{k}.$$

Substituting (6. 21) in (6. 8) and (6. 12) we obtain

(6. 22) $$(I - M)\overline{dY} = dE$$
$$(I - M)\bar{k} = e$$

which, when both sides are multiplied through by $(I - M)^{-1}$, is the same as (6. 18). If we substitute (6. 20) in (6. 8) and (6. 12) we obtain

(6. 23)
$$dY(t) = dE + M[\overline{dY} + d\hat{Y}(t-1)] = dE + M\overline{dY} + Md\hat{Y}(t-1)$$
$$k(t) = e + M[\bar{k} + \hat{k}(t-1)] = e + Mk + M\hat{k}(t-1),$$

the first part of which is the stationary part

(6. 24) $$\overline{dY} = dE + M\overline{dY}$$
$$\bar{k} = e + M\bar{k},$$

and the second part of which is the transient part

(6. 25) $$d\hat{Y}(t) = Md\hat{Y}(t-1)$$
$$\hat{k}(t) = M\hat{k}(t-1),$$

which is the system of associated homogeneous equations to (6. 8) and (6. 12).

2. Since the matrix solution (6. 17) of the multi-sector multiplier consists of two parts—a stationary and a transient part—as shown in (6. 19), the scalar solution of the multi-sector multiplier (the solution for the receipts or multiplier of any sector i, in scalar form) is the sum of the scalar solutions of

the static system of equations (6.24) and the dynamic system of equations (6.25). This may be expressed by

(6.26) $$dY_i(t) = \overline{dY_i} + \hat{dY_i}(t)$$

$$k_i(t) = \bar{k}_i + \hat{k}_i(t).$$

We shall first derive the scalar solution of the static system (6.24).

Equations (6.24), when written out, become

(6.27) $$\begin{cases} \overline{dY}_1 = dE_1 + {}_1E'_1\overline{dY}_1 + {}_2E'_1\overline{dY}_2 + \cdots + {}_nE'_1\overline{dY}_n \\ \overline{dY}_2 = dE_2 + {}_1E'_2\overline{dY}_1 + {}_2E'_2\overline{dY}_2 + \cdots + {}_nE'_2\overline{dY}_n \\ \\ \overline{dY}_n = dE_n + {}_1E'_n\overline{dY}_1 + {}_2E'_n\overline{dY}_2 + \cdots + {}_nE'_n\overline{dY}_n \end{cases}$$

and the equivalent system

(6.28) $$\begin{cases} \bar{k}_1 = e_1 + {}_1E'_1\bar{k}_1 + {}_2E'_1\bar{k}_2 + \cdots + {}_nE'_1\bar{k}_n \\ \bar{k}_2 = e_2 + {}_1E'_2\bar{k}_1 + {}_2E'_2\bar{k}_2 + \cdots + {}_nE'_2\bar{k}_n \\ \\ \bar{k}_n = e_n + {}_1E'_n\bar{k}_1 + {}_2E'_n\bar{k}_2 + \cdots + {}_nE'_n\bar{k}_n \end{cases}$$

In their rearranged form, these become

(6.29) $$\begin{cases} (1 - {}_1E'_1)\overline{dY}_1 - {}_2E'_1\overline{dY}_2 - \cdots - {}_nE'_1\overline{dY}_n = dE_1 \\ - {}_1E'_2\overline{dY}_1 + (1 - {}_2E'_2)\overline{dY}_2 - \cdots - {}_nE'_2\overline{dY}_n = dE_2 \\ \\ - {}_1E'_n dY_1 - {}_2E'_n dY_2 - \cdots + (1 - {}_nE'_n)\overline{dY}_n = dE_n \end{cases}$$

and

(6.30) $$\begin{cases} (1 - {}_1E'_1)\bar{k}_1 - {}_2E'_1\bar{k}_2 - \cdots - {}_nE'_1\bar{k}_n = e_1 \\ - {}_1E'_2\bar{k}_1 + (1 - {}_2E'_2)\bar{k}_2 - \cdots - {}_nE'_2\bar{k}_n = e_2 \\ \\ - {}_1E'_n\bar{k}_1 - {}_2E'_n\bar{k}_2 - \cdots + (1 - {}_nE'_n)\bar{k}_n = e_n. \end{cases}$$

By Cramer's rule, the final (or equilibrium) values of receipts and multipliers may readily be determined. From (6.29) we obtain the solution

4

$$(6.31) \quad \overline{dY_i} = \frac{\begin{vmatrix} 1 - {}_1E'_1 & - {}_2E'_1 & \cdots & dE_1 & \cdots & - {}_nE'_1 \\ - {}_1E'_2 & 1 - {}_2E'_2 & \cdots & dE_2 & \cdots & - {}_nE'_2 \\ \cdot & \cdot & \cdot & \cdot & \cdot & \cdot \\ - {}_1E'_n & - {}_2E'_n & \cdots & dE_n & \cdots & 1 - {}_nE'_n \end{vmatrix}}{\begin{vmatrix} 1 - {}_1E'_1 & - {}_2E'_1 & \cdots & - {}_iE'_1 & \cdots & - {}_nE'_1 \\ - {}_1E'_2 & 1 - {}_2E'_2 & \cdots & - {}_iE'_2 & \cdots & - {}_nE'_2 \\ \cdot & \cdot & \cdot & \cdot & \cdot & \cdot \\ - {}_1E'_n & - {}_2E'_n & \cdots & - {}_iE'_n & \cdots & 1 - {}_nE'_n \end{vmatrix}}$$

which may be written more briefly

$$(6.32) \qquad \overline{dY_i} = \frac{d\Delta_i}{\Delta}$$

where Δ is the determinant of $I - M$ and $d\Delta_i$ is the determinant formed by substituting dE in the i-th column of $I - M$. From (6.30) we obtain

$$(6.33) \quad \bar{k}_i = \frac{\begin{vmatrix} 1 - {}_1E'_1 & - {}_2E'_1 & \cdots & e_1 & \cdots & - {}_nE'_1 \\ - {}_1E'_2 & 1 - {}_2E'_2 & \cdots & e_2 & \cdots & - {}_nE'_2 \\ \cdot & \cdot & \cdot & \cdot & \cdot & \cdot \\ - {}_1E'_n & - {}_2E'_n & \cdots & e_n & \cdots & 1 - {}_nE'_n \end{vmatrix}}{\begin{vmatrix} 1 - {}_1E'_1 & - {}_2E'_1 & \cdots & - {}_iE'_1 & \cdots & - {}_nE'_1 \\ - {}_1E'_2 & 1 - {}_2E'_2 & \cdots & - {}_iE'_2 & \cdots & - {}_nE'_2 \\ \cdot & \cdot & \cdot & \cdot & \cdot & \cdot \\ - {}_1E'_n & - {}_2E'_n & \cdots & - {}_iE'_n & \cdots & 1 - {}_nE'_n \end{vmatrix}}$$

or, more briefly,

$$(6.34) \qquad \bar{k}_i = \frac{\Delta'_i}{\Delta}$$

where Δ'_i is the determinant of the matrix formed by substituting e in the i-th column of $I - M$. This is the static multiplier.

The receipts and multiplier for a group of s sectors are given by

$$(6.35) \qquad \sum_{i=1}^{s} \overline{dY_i} = \frac{\sum_{i=1}^{s} d\Delta_i}{\Delta}$$

$$\sum_{i=1}^{s} \bar{k}_i = \frac{\sum_{i=1}^{s} \Delta'_i}{\Delta}.$$

If sectors 1 to s are Households, (6.35) gives us the static national income multiplier; if they are Households and Business (and Government, if governments have non-zero marginal propensities to spend), (6.35) is the static total transactions multiplier. Finance and fictitious collecting agencies should not be included in these summations.

Some special cases of the static multi-sector multiplier may be noted. In the case in which $e_1 = 1$ and all the other e_i's are zero, (6.31) and (6.33) become (for sector 1)

$$(6.36) \qquad \frac{dY_1}{dE_1} = \frac{1}{1 - \sum_{i=1}^{n} (C_i/C_1)_1 E'_i}$$

where C_i is the cofactor of the i-th element in the first column of $I - M$. Other special cases are derived by giving various forms to the vector e. Thus, the effect on sector 1's receipts of disbursement to sector 2 is given by setting $e_2 = 1$ and all other e_i's $= 0$; the effect on 1's receipts of an "export" from 1 to 2 is given by setting $e_1 = 1$, $e_2 = -1$, and all the other e_i's $= 0$; similarly the effect of an export from 2 to 3 is given by setting $e_2 = 1$, $e_3 = -1$, and all the other e_i's $= 0$. If the sectors are regions, the effect on 1's income of an autonomous expenditure in 1 which is partly devoted to expenditure on materials and profits accruing to the other $n - 1$ regions, is evaluated by assigning the appropriate values to the e_i's, where $\sum_{i=1}^{n} e_i = 1$. The ultimate effect of any autonomous redistribution of income on income as a whole is evaluated by substituting the appropriate values for the e_i's in (6.35), where $\sum_{i=1}^{n} e_i = 0$.

3. We come now to the scalar solution of the associated homogeneous system (6.25) which is the transient (dynamic) part of the systems (6.8) and (6.12). This solution may be found with the assistance of an operator λ, which turns the last period's receipts or multiplier vector into the present period's receipts or multiplier vector, as follows:

(6.37)
$$\lambda \hat{dY}(t-1) = \hat{dY}(t)$$
$$\lambda \hat{k}(t-1) = \hat{k}(t).$$

Applying this operator to (6.25), we obtain

(6.38)
$$\lambda \hat{dY}(t-1) = M \hat{dY}(t-1)$$
$$\lambda \hat{k}(t-1) = M \hat{k}(t-1).$$

Written out, the first of these equations becomes

(6.39)
$$\begin{cases} \lambda \hat{dY}_1(t-1) = {}_1E'_1 \hat{dY}_1(t-1) + {}_2E'_1 \hat{dY}_2(t-1) + \cdots + {}_nE'_1 \hat{dY}_n(t-1) \\ \lambda \hat{dY}_2(t-1) = {}_1E'_2 \hat{dY}_1(t-1) + {}_2E'_2 \hat{dY}_2(t-1) + \cdots + {}_nE'_2 \hat{dY}_n(t-1) \\ \\ \lambda \hat{dY}_n(t-1) = {}_1E'_n \hat{dY}_1(t-1) + {}_2E'_n \hat{dY}_2(t-1) + \cdots + {}_nE'_n \hat{dY}_n(t-1) \end{cases}$$

which may be rearranged in the form

(6.40)
$$\begin{cases} (\lambda - {}_1E'_1)\hat{dY}_1(t-1) - {}_2E'_1\hat{dY}_2(t-1) - \cdots - {}_nE'_1\hat{dY}_n(t-1) = 0 \\ - {}_1E'_2\hat{dY}_1(t-1) + (\lambda - {}_2E'_2)\hat{dY}_2(t-1) - \cdots - {}_nE'_2\hat{dY}_n(t-1) \\ \\ - {}_1E'_n\hat{dY}_1(t-1) - {}_2E'_n\hat{dY}_2(t-1) - \cdots + (\lambda - {}_nE'_n)\hat{dY}_n(t-1) \end{cases}$$

and written

(6.41)
$$\begin{bmatrix} \lambda - {}_1E'_1 & - {}_2E'_1 \cdots & - {}_nE'_1 \\ - {}_1E'_2 & \lambda - {}_2E'_2 \cdots & - {}_nE'_2 \\ \vdots & & \\ - {}_1E'_n & - {}_2E'_n \cdots \lambda - {}_nE'_n \end{bmatrix} \begin{bmatrix} \hat{dY}_1(t-1) \\ \hat{dY}_2(t-1) \\ \vdots \\ \hat{dY}_n(t-1) \end{bmatrix} = \begin{bmatrix} 0 \\ 0 \\ \vdots \\ 0 \end{bmatrix}.$$

(6.41) gives us the matric equations

(6.42)
$$(I\lambda - M)\hat{dY}(t-1) = 0$$
$$(I\lambda - M)\hat{k}(t-1) = 0.$$

One possible solution is immediately apparent, namely the solution

(6.43)
$$\hat{dY}(t) = \hat{dY}(t-1) = 0$$
$$\hat{k}(t) = \hat{k}(t-1) = 0.$$

But this can be true only if

(6. 44)
$$dE = 0 \qquad\qquad e = 0.$$

This is therefore a trivial and uninteresting solution. Consequently we reject this solution and conclude that the matrix $I\lambda - M$ is the annihilator of the vectors $d\hat{Y}(t-1)$ and $\hat{k}(t-1)$, and is therefore singular. In other words, the determinant of $I\lambda - M$ must vanish:

(6. 45)
$$|I\lambda - M| \equiv \begin{vmatrix} \lambda - {}_1E'_1 & - {}_2E'_1 \cdots & - {}_nE'_1 \\ - {}_1E'_2 & \lambda - {}_2E'_2 \cdots & - {}_nE'_2 \\ \cdot & \cdots & \cdot \\ - {}_1E'_n & - {}_2E'_n \cdots & \lambda - {}_nE'_n \end{vmatrix} = 0.$$

Equation (6. 45) is known as the characteristic equation of the system of equations (6. 6) and (6. 10); in its explicit form it is written

(6. 46)
$$\sum_{s=0}^{n} (-1)^s D_s \lambda^{n-s} \equiv \lambda^n - D_1{}^{n-1} + D_2{}^{n-2}$$
$$- \cdots + (-1)^{n-1} D_{n-1} \lambda + (-1)^n D_n = 0$$

where D_s is the sum of the $\dfrac{n!}{s!(n-s)!}$ s-th-order minors symmetric about the principal diagonal of M, D_n is the determinant of M, and $D_0 = 1$. The roots of this polynomial are the characteristic or latent roots of the matrix M. For example, when $n = 3$, we have

(6. 47)
$$D_0 = 1$$

$$D_1 = {}_1E'_1 + {}_2E'_2 + {}_3E'_3$$

$$D_2 = \begin{vmatrix} {}_1E'_1 & {}_2E'_1 \\ {}_1E'_2 & {}_2E'_2 \end{vmatrix} + \begin{vmatrix} {}_2E'_2 & {}_3E'_2 \\ {}_2E'_3 & {}_3E'_3 \end{vmatrix} + \begin{vmatrix} {}_1E'_1 & {}_3E'_1 \\ {}_1E'_3 & {}_3E'_3 \end{vmatrix}$$

$$D_3 = \begin{vmatrix} {}_1E'_1 & {}_2E'_1 & {}_3E'_1 \\ {}_1E'_2 & {}_2E'_2 & {}_3E'_2 \\ {}_1E'_3 & {}_2E'_3 & {}_3E'_3 \end{vmatrix}.$$

It will be noted that if we set $\lambda = 1$, we obtain the expansion

(6. 48)
$$|I - M| \equiv \Delta = 1 - D_1 + D_2$$
$$- \cdots + (-1)^{n-1} D_{n-1} + (-1)^n D_n.$$

Now (6.46) will be recognized as the characteristic polynomial of the n-th-order difference equations

(6.49) $\displaystyle\sum_{s=0}^{n}(-1)^s D_s \hat{dY}_i(t-s)$

$$\equiv \hat{dY}_i(t) - D_1 \hat{dY}_i(t-1) + D_2 \hat{dY}_i(t-2)$$

$$-\cdots + (-1)^n D_n \hat{dY}_i(t-n) = 0$$

$$\sum_{s=0}^{n}(-1)^s D_s \hat{k}_i(t-s)$$

$$\equiv \hat{k}_i(t) - D_1 \hat{k}_i(t-1) + D_2 \hat{k}_i(t-2)$$

$$-\cdots + (-1)^n D_n \hat{k}_i(t-n) = 0$$

whose solutions are in the forms

(6.50) $\displaystyle \hat{dY}_i(t) = \sum_{j=1}^{n} g_{ij}\lambda_j{}^t$ $\displaystyle \hat{k}_i(t) = \sum_{j=1}^{n} c_{ij}\lambda_j{}^t$

where the λ_j's are the roots of (6.46), and where the coefficients g_{ij} and c_{ij} are arbitrary constants whose values we shall determine in §5 of this section.

4. We may now derive the general scalar solution of the multi-sector multiplier. It follows from (6.32) and (6.34) that

(6.51) $\Delta \overline{dY}_i = d\Delta_i$ $\Delta \bar{k}_i = \Delta'_i$

Because of the expansion (6.48), (6.51) may be expressed

(6.52) $\displaystyle\sum_{s=0}^{n}(-1)^s D_s \overline{dY}_i = d\Delta_i$

$$\sum_{s=0}^{n}(-1) D_s \bar{k}_i = \Delta'_i$$

or, written out,

(6.53) $\overline{dY}_i - D_1\overline{dY}_i + D_2\overline{dY}_i - \cdots + (-1)^n D_n\overline{dY}_i = d\Delta_i$

$$\bar{k}_i - D_1\bar{k}_i + D_2\bar{k}_i - \cdots + (-1)^n D_n\bar{k}_i = \Delta'_i.$$

Since, as shown in (6.26), the general scalar solution is the sum of the static and dynamic scalar solutions, we may add (6.49) and (6.35) to obtain:

(6.54) $\sum_{s=0}^{n}(-1)^{s}D_{s}dY_{i}(t-s)\equiv dY_{i}(t)-D_{1}dY_{i}(t-1)$

$$+ D_{2}dY_{i}(t-2)-\cdots+(-1)^{n}D_{n}dY_{i}(t-n) = d\Delta_{i}$$

$\sum_{s=0}^{n}(-1)^{s}D_{s}k_{i}(t-s)\equiv k_{i}(t)-D_{1}k_{i}(t-1)$

$$+ D_{2}k_{i}(t-2)-\cdots+(-1)^{n}D_{n}k_{i}(t-n) = \Delta'_{i}.$$

These n-th-order scalar difference equations (6.54) are completely equivalent to the first-order equations (6.8) and (6.12). They are simply the representation of (6.8) and (6.12) in scalar form. The general scalar solution of the multi-sector multiplier is therefore the solution of (6.54). This solution is

(6.55)
$$dY_{i}(t) = \frac{d\Delta_{i}}{\Delta} + \sum_{j=1}^{n} g_{ij}\lambda_{j}^{t}$$

$$k_{i}(t) = \frac{\Delta'_{i}}{\Delta} + \sum_{j=1}^{n} c_{ij}\lambda_{j}^{t},$$

which is the sum of the stationary solution (6.32) and (6.34) and the transient solution (6.50). If the absolute value of every λ_{j} is less than unity, (6.55) will converge to (6.32) and (6.34) as t approaches infinity. There is also a trivial case in which all the λ_{j}'s are equal to zero, and λ is the null operator; this means that the equilibrium value is reached instantaneously, which can be true if reactions are instantaneous (and, as a special, and even more trivial, case of this, if marginal propensities to spend all are zero), so that disbursements follow receipts without any lag.

It follows from (6.55) that we may write

(6.56)
$$\sum_{i=1}^{s} dY_{i}(t) = \sum_{i=1}^{s} d\Delta_{i}/\Delta + \sum_{i=1}^{s}\sum_{j=1}^{n} g_{ij}\lambda_{j}^{t}$$

$$\sum_{i=1}^{s} k_{i}(t) = \sum_{i=1}^{s} \Delta'_{i}/\Delta + \sum_{i=1}^{s}\sum_{j=1}^{n} c_{ij}\lambda_{j}^{t}$$

which may be taken as the income or transactions multipliers, or the multipliers for any other group of sectors, depending upon what sectors are included from 1 to s.

It is sometimes convenient to write (6.55) and (6.56) in a slightly different form. (6.55) may be written

(6.57)
$$dY_i(t) = \frac{d\Delta_i}{\Delta} (1 + \sum_{j=1}^{n} \gamma_{ij}\lambda_j{}^t)$$

$$k_i(t) = \frac{\Delta'_i}{\Delta} (1 + \sum_{j=1}^{n} \kappa_{ij}\lambda_j{}^t)$$

where

(6.58)
$$\gamma_{ij} = \frac{g_{ij}}{d\Delta_i/\Delta} \qquad \kappa_{ij} = \frac{c_{ij}}{\Delta'_i/\Delta}$$

and (6.56) may be written

(6.59)
$$\sum_{i=1}^{s} dY_i(t) = \frac{\sum_{i=1}^{s} d\Delta_i}{\Delta} (1 + \sum_{j=1}^{n} G_j\lambda_j{}^t)$$

$$\sum_{i=1}^{s} k_i(t) = \frac{\sum_{i=1}^{s} \Delta'_i}{\Delta} (1 + \sum_{j=1}^{n} K_j\lambda_j{}^t)$$

where

(6.60)
$$G_j = \frac{\sum_{i=1}^{s} g_{ij}}{\sum_{i=1}^{s} d\Delta_i/\Delta}$$

$$K_j = \frac{\sum_{i=1}^{s} c_{ij}}{\sum_{i=1}^{s} \Delta'_i/\Delta}.$$

It now remains to evaluate these arbitrary constants.

5. From (6.55), (6.56), (6.57), and (6.59), we may set up, by giving to t the successive values $0, 1, \cdots, n-1$, their corresponding systems of equations, as follows:

(6.61)

$$
\begin{aligned}
g_{i1} \quad &+ g_{i2} \quad &+ g_{i3} \quad &+ \cdots + g_{in} \quad &= dY_i(0) \quad &- d\Delta_i/\Delta \\
g_{i1}\lambda_1 \quad &+ g_{i2}\lambda_2 \quad &+ g_{i3}\lambda_3 \quad &+ \cdots + g_{in}\lambda_n \quad &= dY_i(1) \quad &- d\Delta_i/\Delta \\
g_{i1}\lambda_1{}^2 \quad &+ g_{i2}\lambda_2{}^2 \quad &+ g_{i3}\lambda_3{}^2 \quad &+ \cdots + g_{in}\lambda_n{}^2 \quad &= dY_i(2) \quad &- d\Delta_i/\Delta \\
\end{aligned}
$$

$$g_{i1}\lambda_1{}^{n-1} + g_{i2}\lambda_2{}^{n-1} + g_{i3}\lambda_3{}^{n-1} + \cdots + g_{in}\lambda_n{}^{n-1} = dY_i(n-1) - d\Delta_i/\Delta.$$

(6.61) may be written in matric form:

(6. 62)

$$
\begin{bmatrix}
1 & 1 & 1 & \cdots 1 \\
\lambda_1 & \lambda_2 & \lambda_3 & \cdots \lambda_n \\
\lambda_1{}^2 & \lambda_2{}^2 & \lambda_3{}^2 & \cdots \lambda_n{}^2 \\
. & . & . & . \\
\lambda_1{}^{n-1} & \lambda_2{}^{n-1} & \lambda_3{}^{n-1} & \cdots \lambda_n{}^{n-1}
\end{bmatrix}
\begin{bmatrix}
g_{i1} \\
g_{i2} \\
g_{i3} \\
. \\
g_{in}
\end{bmatrix}
=
\begin{bmatrix}
dY_i(0) & \overline{-dY_i} \\
dY_i(1) & \overline{-dY_i} \\
dY_i(2) & \overline{-dY_i} \\
. & . \\
dY_i(n-1) & \overline{-dY_i}
\end{bmatrix}.
$$

Similarly we have

(6. 63)

$$
\begin{bmatrix}
1 & 1 & 1 & \cdots 1 \\
\lambda_1 & \lambda_2 & \lambda_3 & \cdots \lambda_n \\
\lambda_1{}^2 & \lambda_2{}^2 & \lambda_3{}^2 & \cdots \lambda_n{}^2 \\
. & . & . & . \\
\lambda_1{}^{n-1} & \lambda_2{}^{n-1} & \lambda_3{}^{n-1} & \cdots \lambda_n{}^{n-1}
\end{bmatrix}
\begin{bmatrix}
c_{i1} \\
c_{i2} \\
c_{i3} \\
. \\
c_{in}
\end{bmatrix}
=
\begin{bmatrix}
k_i(0) & -\overline{k}_i \\
k_i(1) & -\overline{k}_i \\
k_i(2) & -\overline{k}_i \\
. & . \\
k_i(n-1) & -\overline{k}_i
\end{bmatrix}.
$$

In the same way, we obtain from (6. 56) the equations

(6. 64)

$$
\begin{bmatrix}
1 & 1 & 1 & \cdots 1 \\
\lambda_1 & \lambda_2 & \lambda_3 & \cdots \lambda_n \\
\lambda_1{}^2 & \lambda_2{}^2 & \lambda_3{}^2 & \cdots \lambda_n{}^2 \\
. & . & . & . \\
\lambda_1{}^{n-1} & \lambda_2{}^{n-1} & \lambda_3{}^{n-1} & \cdots \lambda_n{}^{n-1}
\end{bmatrix}
\begin{bmatrix}
\sum_{i=1}^{s} g_{i1} \\
\sum_{i=1}^{s} g_{i2} \\
\sum_{i=1}^{s} g_{i3} \\
. \\
\sum_{i=1}^{s} g_{in}
\end{bmatrix}
=
\begin{bmatrix}
\sum_{i=1}^{s} dY_i(0) & -\sum_{i=1}^{s} \overline{dY}_i \\
\sum_{i=1}^{s} dY_i(1) & -\sum_{i=1}^{s} \overline{dY}_i \\
\sum_{i=1}^{s} dY_i(2) & -\sum_{i=1}^{s} \overline{dY}_i \\
. & . \\
\sum_{i=1}^{s} dY_i(n-1) & -\sum_{i=1}^{s} \overline{dY}_i
\end{bmatrix}
$$

and

(6. 65)

$$
\begin{bmatrix}
1 & 1 & 1 & \cdots 1 \\
\lambda_1 & \lambda_2 & \lambda_3 & \cdots \lambda_n \\
\lambda_1{}^2 & \lambda_2{}^2 & \lambda_3{}^2 & \cdots \lambda_n{}^2 \\
. & . & . & . \\
\lambda_1{}^{n-1} & \lambda_2{}^{n-1} & \lambda_3{}^{n-1} & \cdots \lambda_n{}^{n-1}
\end{bmatrix}
\begin{bmatrix}
\sum_{i=1}^{s} c_{i1} \\
\sum_{i=1}^{s} c_{i2} \\
\sum_{i=1}^{s} c_{i3} \\
. \\
\sum_{i=1}^{s} c_{in}
\end{bmatrix}
=
\begin{bmatrix}
\sum_{i=1}^{s} k_i(0) & -\sum_{i=1}^{s} \overline{k}_i \\
\sum_{i=1}^{s} k_i(1) & -\sum_{i=1}^{s} \overline{k}_i \\
\sum_{i=1}^{s} k_i(2) & -\sum_{i=1}^{s} \overline{k}_i \\
. & . \\
\sum_{i=1}^{s} k_i(n-1) & -\sum_{i=1}^{s} \overline{k}_i
\end{bmatrix}.
$$

Again, we have from (6.57) the equations

(6.66)

$$
\begin{bmatrix}
1 & 1 & 1 & \cdots & 1 \\
\lambda_1 & \lambda_2 & \lambda_3 & \cdots & \lambda_n \\
\lambda_1{}^2 & \lambda_2{}^2 & \lambda_3{}^2 & \cdots & \lambda_n{}^2 \\
\cdot & \cdot & \cdot & \cdot & \cdot \\
\lambda_1{}^{n-1} & \lambda_2{}^{n-1} & \lambda_3{}^{n-1} & \cdots & \lambda_n{}^{n-1}
\end{bmatrix}
\begin{bmatrix}
\gamma_{i1} \\
\gamma_{i2} \\
\gamma_{i3} \\
\cdot \\
\gamma_{in}
\end{bmatrix}
=
\begin{bmatrix}
dY_i(0)/\overline{dY_i} & -1 \\
dY_i(1)/\overline{dY_i} & -1 \\
dY_i(2)/\overline{dY_i} & -1 \\
\cdot & \cdot \\
dY_i(n-1)/\overline{dY_i} & -1
\end{bmatrix}
$$

and

(6.67)

$$
\begin{bmatrix}
1 & 1 & 1 & \cdots & 1 \\
\lambda_1 & \lambda_2 & \lambda_3 & \cdots & \lambda_n \\
\lambda_1{}^2 & \lambda_2{}^2 & \lambda_3{}^2 & \cdots & \lambda_n{}^2 \\
\cdot & \cdot & \cdot & \cdot & \cdot \\
\lambda_1{}^{n-1} & \lambda_2{}^{n-1} & \lambda_3{}^{n-1} & \cdots & \lambda_n{}^{n-1}
\end{bmatrix}
\begin{bmatrix}
\kappa_{i1} \\
\kappa_{i2} \\
\kappa_{i3} \\
\cdot \\
\kappa_{in}
\end{bmatrix}
=
\begin{bmatrix}
k_i(0)/\bar{k}_i & -1 \\
k_i(1)/\bar{k}_i & -1 \\
k_i(2)/\bar{k}_i & -1 \\
\cdot & \cdot \\
k_i(n-1)/\bar{k}_i & -1
\end{bmatrix}
$$

and from (6.59) we have

(6.68)

$$
\begin{bmatrix}
1 & 1 & 1 & \cdots & 1 \\
\lambda_1 & \lambda_2 & \lambda_3 & \cdots & \lambda_n \\
\lambda_1{}^2 & \lambda_2{}^2 & \lambda_3{}^2 & \cdots & \lambda_n{}^2 \\
\cdot & \cdot & \cdot & \cdot & \cdot \\
\lambda_1{}^{n-1} & \lambda_2{}^{n-1} & \lambda_3{}^{n-1} & \cdots & \lambda_n{}^{n-1}
\end{bmatrix}
\begin{bmatrix}
G_1 \\
G_2 \\
G_3 \\
\cdot \\
G_n
\end{bmatrix}
=
\begin{bmatrix}
\sum_{i=1}^{s} dY_i(0)/\sum_{i=1}^{s} \overline{dY_i} & -1 \\
\sum_{i=1}^{s} dY_i(1)/\sum_{i=1}^{s} \overline{dY_i} & -1 \\
\sum_{i=1}^{s} dY_i(2)/\sum_{i=1}^{s} \overline{dY_i} & -1 \\
\cdot & \cdot \\
\sum_{i=1}^{s} dY_i(n-1)/\sum_{i=1}^{s} \overline{dY_i} & -1
\end{bmatrix}
$$

and

(6. 69)

$$
\begin{bmatrix}
1 & 1 & 1 & \cdots & 1 \\
\lambda_1 & \lambda_2 & \lambda_3 & \cdots & \lambda_n \\
\lambda_1^2 & \lambda_2^2 & \lambda_3^2 & \cdots & \lambda_n^2 \\
\cdot & \cdot & \cdot & \cdot & \cdot & \cdot \\
\lambda_1^{n-1} & \lambda_2^{n-1} & \lambda_3^{n-1} & \cdots & \lambda_n^{n-1}
\end{bmatrix}
\begin{bmatrix}
K_1 \\
K_2 \\
K_3 \\
\cdot \\
K_n
\end{bmatrix}
=
\begin{bmatrix}
\sum_{i=1}^{s} k_i(0) / \sum_{i=1}^{s} \bar{k}_i & -1 \\
\sum_{i=1}^{s} k_i(1) / \sum_{i=1}^{s} \bar{k}_i & -1 \\
\sum_{i=1}^{s} k_i(2) / \sum_{i=1}^{s} \bar{k}_i & -1 \\
\cdot \cdot \cdot \cdot \cdot \cdot \\
\sum_{i=1}^{s} k_i(n-1) / \sum_{i=1}^{s} \bar{k}_i - 1
\end{bmatrix}.
$$

The matrix which appears in equations (6.62) to (6.69) is known as the Vandermonde matrix, and may be denoted by the symbol V. In each case, the Vandermonde matrix operates on a vector of arbitrary constants—a typical one of which may be denoted by ω—to produce a vector whose elements are the time-path of receipts or of the multiplier, up to time $n-1$, expressed either as a deviation from or as a proportion to the equilibrium value of receipts or of the multiplier. For brevity, we may describe this vector as the time-path vector, a typical one of which is represented by τ. In general, we have the relationship

(6. 70) $$V\omega = \tau$$

so that the arbitrary constants are determined from the roots and from the time-path: [5]

(6. 71) $$\omega = V^{-1}\tau.$$

A typical arbitrary constant—the coefficient of the j-th latent root—is evaluated, by Cramer's rule, as follows:

---

[5] We shall not consider here the case of repeated roots, in which V has no inverse. For this case the reader may consult P. A. Samuelson, *Foundations of Economic Analysis* (Cambridge, Mass., 1948), Appendix B.

$$(6.72) \qquad \omega_j = \frac{\begin{vmatrix} 1 & 1 & \cdots \tau(0) & \cdots 1 \\ \lambda_1 & \lambda_2 & \cdots \tau(1) & \cdots \lambda_n \\ \cdot & \cdot & \cdots & \cdot \\ \lambda_1{}^{n-1} & \lambda_2{}^{n-1} \cdots & \tau(n-1) \cdots & \lambda_n{}^{n-1} \end{vmatrix}}{\begin{vmatrix} 1 & 1 & \cdots 1 & \cdots 1 \\ \lambda_1 & \lambda_2 & \cdots \lambda_j & \cdots \lambda_n \\ \cdot & \cdot & \cdots & \cdot \\ \lambda_1{}^{n-1} & \lambda_2{}^{n-1} \cdots & \lambda_j{}^{n-1} \cdots & \lambda_n{}^{n-1} \end{vmatrix}} \ .$$

Evidently, the time-path—up to $n-1$ periods—must already be known if the arbitrary constants are to be evaluated. The time-path can be evaluated directly from equations (6.15) and (6.16). In the case of $n \leq 2$ the time-path need not be calculated, since it follows from (6.13) and (6.14).

The usefulness of the scalar solution (6.55) (and the equivalent or related solutions (6.56), (6.57), and (6.59)) may well be questioned, since the time-path of receipts or of the multiplier must already be calculated from the matrix solution (6.15) and (6.16) up to the $(n-1)$-th period, before the scalar solution is determinate. Since it is the time-path with which we are usually concerned, once it is evaluated there is little purpose in calculating the arbitrary constants. We shall see in the next chapter, nevertheless, that many useful theorems and observations may be derived from the scalar solution, particularly in relation to the study of oscillations.

6. Before we leave the scalar solution of the multiplier, we must analyze the case of complex roots.[6] The prototype of the solutions (6.55), (6.56), (6.57) and (6.59) may be written

$$(6.73) \qquad \sum_{j=1}^{n} \omega_j \lambda_j{}^t = \tau(t)$$

A number of roots may be complex, and consequently a number of arbitrary constants may be complex; but we know that the time-path $\tau(t)$ cannot be complex. Any complex element $\omega_s \lambda_s{}^t$ must therefore be transformed into a real form.

It is known from a fundamental theorem of algebra that

---

[6] I am indebted to Dr. Ta-Chung Liu for advice in the analysis which follows.

complex roots always occur in pairs of complex conjugates. Let the s-th and $(s+1)$-th roots be such a pair of conjugate complex numbers. Then we may write

$$(6.74) \qquad \begin{aligned} \lambda_s &= u_s + i v_s \\ \lambda_{s+1} &= \bar{\lambda}_s = u_s - i v_s \end{aligned} \qquad i = \sqrt{-1}$$

where a bar must here be understood to denote a complex conjugate. Diagrammatically these roots may be portrayed as vectors in the complex plane, where real numbers are measured along the horizontal axis, and imaginary numbers along the vertical axis, as in Figure 10.

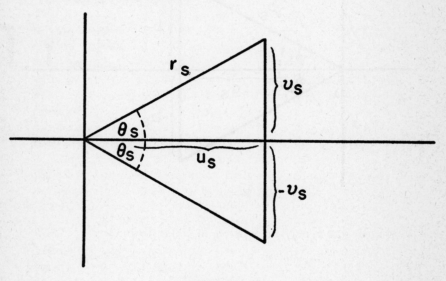

Figure 10.

Hence u and v may be written in polar form

$$(6.75) \qquad u_s = r_s \cos \theta_s \qquad\qquad v_s = r_s \sin \theta_s$$

where

$$(6.76) \qquad r_s = \sqrt{u_s^2 + v_s^2} \qquad\qquad \theta_s = v_s / u_s$$

so that the roots λ_s and $\bar{\lambda}_s$ may be written in polar coordinates:

$$(6.77) \qquad \lambda_s = r_s(\cos \theta + i \sin \theta_s) \qquad \bar{\lambda}_s = r_s(\cos \theta - i \sin \theta_s).$$

From (6.72) the corresponding arbitrary constants may be evaluated. These will always be found to be complex conjugates,[7] of the form

(6.78) $\qquad\qquad \omega_s = a_s + ib_s \qquad\qquad \omega_{s+1} = \bar{\omega}_s = a_s - ib_s.$

The arbitrary constants may likewise be represented in diagrammatical form in the complex plane, as in Figure 11:

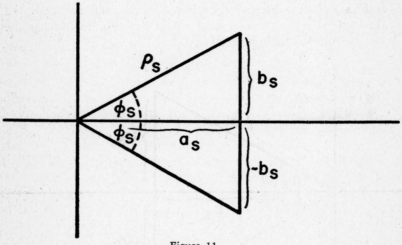

Figure 11.

so that a and b may be written in polar form

(6.79) $\qquad\qquad a_s = \rho_s \cos \phi_s \qquad\qquad b_s = \rho_s \sin \phi_s$

where

(6.80) $\qquad\qquad \rho_s = \sqrt{a_s^2 + b_s^2} \qquad\qquad \phi_s = b_s/a_s$

and the constants ω_s and $\bar{\omega}_s$ may be written in polar coordinates

(6.81)

$$\omega_s = \rho_s(\cos \phi_s + i \sin \phi_s)$$

$$\bar{\omega}_s = \rho_s(\cos \phi_s - i \sin \phi_s).$$

[7] As a special case of this, they may be equal, that is, their imaginary parts may be zero. In this case, the imaginary parts of the corresponding roots will cancel each other out. The reason why they must be complex is simple: if they were not, the time-path would be complex—but that is impossible.

From (6.77) and (6.81) we can now obtain

$$(6.82) \quad \omega_s \lambda_s{}^t + \bar{\omega}_s \bar{\lambda}_s{}^t = \rho_s (\cos \phi_s + i \sin \phi_s) r_s{}^t (\cos \theta_s + i \sin \theta_s)^t$$
$$+ \rho_s (\cos \phi_s - i \sin \phi_s) r_s{}^t (\cos \theta_s - i \sin \theta_s)^t.$$

By De Moivre's Theorem,[8] this reduces to

$$(6.83) \quad \omega_s \lambda_s{}^t + \bar{\omega}_s \bar{\lambda}_s{}^t = \rho_s r_s{}^t \{ (\cos \phi_s + i \sin \phi_s)(\cos t\theta_s + i \sin t\theta_s)$$
$$+ (\cos \phi_s - i \sin \phi_s)(\cos t\theta_s - i \sin t\theta_s) \}.$$

When this is multiplied out, all terms with i cancel out, leaving

$$(6.84) \quad \omega_s \lambda_s{}^t + \bar{\omega}_s \bar{\lambda}_s{}^t = 2\rho_s r_s{}^t (\cos \phi_s \cos t\theta_s - \sin \phi_s \sin t\theta_s)$$
$$= 2\rho_s r_s{}^t \cos(t\theta_s + \phi_s).$$

Any pair of complex conjugate roots, with their arbitrary complex conjugate constants, may be transformed into the form (6.84). Convergence requires that their modulus—r_s—be less than unity in absolute value.

If such is the case, these roots will give rise to damped oscillations. If the modulus is greater than unity, the oscillations will be "explosive."

---

[8] De Moivre's Theorem states that
$$(\cos A \pm i \sin A)^t = \cos tA \pm i \sin tA.$$
A proof may be found in L. E. Dickson, *New First Course in the Theory of Equations* (New York, 1948), pp. 3-4. See also J. R. Hicks, *A Contribution to the Theory of the Trade Cycle* (Oxford, 1950), p. 179.

CHAPTER 7

PROPERTIES OF THE MULTI-SECTOR MULTIPLIER

I. THE CORRESPONDENCE BETWEEN THE STATIC AND DYNAMIC MULTIPLIERS [1]

1. In this section we shall examine the relationship between the static and dynamic multi-sector multipliers, and formulate necessary conditions for the stability of the latter in terms of certain properties of the former.[2]

Stability requires that the roots of (6.46) lie within the unit circle of the complex plane: the absolute value of the modulus of every root must therefore be less than unity. We may relate the values of the roots to properties of the matrix M by means of the property that the i-th-order trace of a matrix is equal to the sum of the products of its latent roots taken i at a time.[3] Two of these traces, the first-order trace (or simply, the trace) and the n-th-order trace (the determinant of M), provide us with the necessary stability conditions.

CONDITION 1. *A necessary condition for stability is that the trace of $I - M$ be positive and less than twice the number of sectors.*

This follows from the fact that

$$(7.1) \qquad \mathrm{tr}\, M = D_1 = \sum_{i=1}^{n} {}_i E'_i = \sum_{i=1}^{n} \lambda_i$$

so that stability requires that

$$(7.2) \qquad -n < \mathrm{tr}\, M < n,$$

that is to say, that the sum of all the sectors' marginal propensities to intraspend, being equal to the sum of the roots,

---

[1] I am greatly indebted to Professor A. H. Clifford for mathematical assistance in this section.

[2] These necessary conditions are an extension to more than two sectors of the necessary and sufficient conditions developed by Metzler in "Underemployment Equilibrium in International Trade."

[3] Cf. A. C. Aitken, *Determinants and Matrices* (5th ed., Edinburgh, 1948), p. 88.

must be less in absolute value than the number of sectors. The average marginal propensity to intraspend must therefore be less than 1 and greater than — 1.

CONDITION 2. *A necessary condition for stability is that the determinant of I — M be positive.*

This follows from the fact that the determinant of M is equal to the product of its latent roots. This is demonstrated in the following theorem.

THEOREM 1. *If the real characteristic roots of M are less than unity, the determinant of I — M is positive.*

PROOF. The determinant of $I — M$ may be reduced to the triangular form:

$$(7.3) \quad |I — P^{-1}MP| = \begin{vmatrix} 1 — \lambda_1 & 0 & 0 & \cdots & 0 \\ — m_{21} & 1 — \lambda_2 & 0 & \cdots & 0 \\ — m_{31} & — m_{32} & 1 — \lambda_3 & \cdots & 0 \\ \vdots & & & & \vdots \\ — m_{n1} & — m_{n2} & — m_{n3} & \cdots & 1 — \lambda_n \end{vmatrix}$$

and is therefore expressible as

$$(7.4) \qquad \Delta = \prod_{i=1}^{n}(1 — \lambda_i)$$

which is obviously positive if every $\lambda_i < 1$. If there are any complex characteristic roots, each complex root λ has its conjugate complex root $\bar{\lambda}$. Hence each complex $1 — \lambda$ must be multiplied by its conjugate $1 — \bar{\lambda}$, the product being positive, for

$$(7.5) \qquad (1 — \lambda)(1 — \bar{\lambda}) = |1 — \lambda|^2 > 0.$$

Complex roots can therefore not make Δ negative. The theorem is therefore proved.

The conditions $— n < \operatorname{tr} M < n$ and $\Delta > 0$ are both necessary conditions for stability, but not sufficient conditions.[4] If either the determinant or the trace of $I — M$ is negative, we know

[4] When $n = 2$, they are also sufficient conditions for monotonic stability; for if one root exceeds unity, $\Delta < 0$, whereas if both exceed unity, $\operatorname{tr} M > 2$. Cf. Metzler, "Underemployment Equilibrium in International Trade," p. 102, equation (7).

that the system is monotonically unstable. It is still possible, however, for the system to be unstable while the two stability conditions hold. For instance, we know that whenever M has negative or complex characteristic roots, and an even number of roots greater than unity, $\Delta > 0$. Thus there may be either monotonic or oscillatory instability without our two conditions reflecting them.

2. We shall now prove that when there is no autonomous transfer of disbursements from one sector or group of sectors of an economy to another, and when no marginal propensity to extraspend is negative, the multiplier for the whole economy must be positive. Let each $dE_i \geq 0$, and at least one $dE_i > 0$; or alternatively, let each $dE_i \leq 0$, and at least one $dE_i < 0$. Then the vector e may be of any conceivable form provided all its element are of the same sign and $\sum_{i=1}^{n} e_i = 1$. Then if the total multiplier $\sum_{i=1}^{n} dY_i / \sum_{i=1}^{n} dE_i$ is to be positive, the column sums of $(I - M)^{-1}$ must all be positive; for if any column sum of $(I - M)^{-1}$ (say the k-th) is not positive, there will exist a vector e (namely the one in which $e_k = 1$ and all the other e_i's are zero) which will make the multiplier nonpositive. Since stability requires that $\Delta > 0$, the condition that the column sums of $(I - M)^{-1}$ be all positive requires under stable conditions, that the column sums of $\mathrm{adj}(I - M)$ be all positive. The following theorem, which is due in its entirety to Professor Clifford, proves that the column sums of $\mathrm{adj}(I - M)$ are positive if marginal propensities to extraspend are not negative and the economy is stable.

THEOREM 2. *Let A be an $n \times n$ matrix satisfying the following two conditions*: (a) *The off-diagonal elements of A are ≥ 0*; (b) *A has no real characteristic root ≥ 1. Then the column sums of* $\mathrm{adj}(I - A)$ *are all positive.*

PROOF. Let $B(t) = I - tA$, where t is a real variable. Then $B(0) = I$, $B(1) = I - A$, and by condition (b)

(7. 6) $\det B(t) > 0$ for $0 \leq t \leq 1$.

For were $\det B(t_1) = 0$, $1/t_1$ would be a characteristic root of A.

Let $c_1(t), c_2(t), \cdots, c_n(t)$ be the column sums of adj $B(t)$. They are polynomials in t all having the value 1 when $t = 0$. We are to show that they are all positive when $t = 1$. If they are not, then let t_1 be the smallest positive root of $c_i(t)$ less than or equal to 1, or define $t_1 = 1$ if $c_i(t)$ has no real root in the interval $(0, 1)$. Let t_0 be the least of the real numbers $t_1, t_2, \cdots, t_n$. Then at least one $c_i(t)$ vanishes for $t = t_0$, while the remaining ones there are positive.

Now observe that

(7.7) $(c_1(t), c_2(t), \cdots, c_n(t)) = (1, 1, \cdots, 1)\,\mathrm{adj}\,B(t)$

hence

(7.8) $(c_1(t), c_2(t), \cdots, c_n(t))B(t)$

$\qquad = (\det B(t), \det B(t), \cdots, \det B(t)).$

Written out, we have

(7.9) $\displaystyle\sum_{i=1}^{n} c_i(t) b_{ij}(t) = \det B(t)$ $\qquad (j = 1, 2, \cdots, n),$

where $b_{ij} = \delta_{ij} - t a_{ij}$.

For simplicity, let us suppose that $c_1(t)$ is one of the $c_i(t)$ which vanish at $t = t_0$. Hence

(7.10) $c_1(t_0) = 0, \qquad c_i(t_0) \geq 0$ $\qquad (i = 2, 3, \cdots, n).$

Consider the first equation in (7.9)

(7.11) $c_1(t)(1 - t a_{11}) - c_2(t) t a_{21} - \cdots - c_n(t) t a_{n1} = \det B(t).$

Set $t = t_0$ in this, and note that t_0 is positive, $c_i(t_0) \geq 0$ for $i \neq 1$, and $a_{i1} \geq 0$ for $i \neq 1$ by condition (a). Hence $c_i(t_0) t_0 a_{i1} \geq 0$ for $i \neq 1$. But $c_1(t_0) = 0$. Hence the left member is ≤ 0, while by (7.6) the right member > 0. We arrive thereby at a contradiction. The theorem is therefore proved.

This theorem shows that negative marginal propensities to intraspend cannot make the multiplier negative. It may be verified by a simple example that negative marginal propensities to extraspend may bring about negative column sums of $\mathrm{adj}(I - M)$ and consequently a negative multiplier. Negative marginal propensities to extraspend will be characteristic of an economy some of whose sectors are in the habit of buying inferior goods from other sectors. Let $M = \begin{bmatrix} 1.1 & 0.1 \\ -0.3 & 0.8 \end{bmatrix}$, so that $I - M = \begin{bmatrix} -0.1 & -0.1 \\ 0.3 & 0.2 \end{bmatrix}$, $\operatorname{tr} M = 1.9$, $\Delta = 0.01$, and $(I - M)^{-1} = \begin{bmatrix} 20 & 10 \\ -30 & -10 \end{bmatrix}$. Then the column sums of $(I - M)^{-1}$ are respectively -10 and 0, so that the multiplier for the whole economy is $-10e_1$. This example shows that the negative marginal propensity to extraspend is accompanied by a greater than unit marginal propensity to intraspend. Thus the multiplier may be stable and negative even though the aggregate marginal propensity to spend is positive in each sector of the economy. The multiplier is positive provided only that marginal propensities to extraspend are positive.

It is therefore possible to have a normal static multiplier corresponding to instability, and an abnormal static multiplier compatible with stabilty. Consequently Professor Samuelson's "correspondence principle" does not always apply.[5]

We shall now develop a further stability condition. First we shall prove the following theorem:

THEOREM 3. *The order of a non-singular matrix is equal to the sum of the products of its i-th-row sum and the i-th-column sum of its inverse.*

PROOF. Let r_i be the i-th-row sum of an $n \times n$ matrix A, and let c'_i be the i-th-column sum of A^{-1}. Then

$$(7.12) \qquad (1, 1, \cdots, 1)A^{-1} = (c'_1, c'_2, \cdots, c'_n)$$

so that

$$(7.13) \qquad (1, 1, \cdots, 1) = (c'_1, c'_2, \cdots, c'_n)A.$$

Taking the row sums of both sides of (7.13), we obtain

$$(7.14) \qquad n = c'_1 r_1 + c'_2 r_2 + \cdots + c'_n r_n$$

which was to be proved.

[5] The correspondence principle, as defined by Samuelson, states that "systems which are well-behaved dynamically tend to be well-behaved from a purely comparative statical viewpoint; likewise those which are unstable give rise to anomalous comparative statical conclusions."—Samuelson, "A Fundamental Multiplier Identity," p. 225.

Applying this theorem to the matrix $(I-M)$ we obtain from (7.13) the equations:

$$
\begin{aligned}
1 &= c'_1(1 - {}_1E'_1) + c'_2(\quad - {}_1E'_2) + \cdots + c'_n(\quad - {}_1E'_n) \\
1 &= c'_1(\quad - {}_2E'_1) + c'_2(1 - {}_2E'_2) + \cdots + c'_n(\quad - {}_2E'_n) \\
&\, \cdot \quad\cdot\quad\cdot\quad\cdot\quad\cdot\quad\cdot\quad\cdot\quad\cdot \\
1 &= c'_1(\quad - {}_nE'_1) + c'_2(\quad - {}_nE'_2) + \cdots + c'_n(1 - {}_nE'_n).
\end{aligned}
$$

(7.15)

Let all marginal propensities to extraspend ≥ 0; then, by Theorem 2, each $c'_i > 0$. Hence the larger the marginal propensities to extraspend, the smaller the r_i's, the larger the c_i's, and the larger the multiplier. Large marginal propensities to extraspend cannot make the multiplier less unstable than small ones. Consequently, any necessary conditions for stability that apply when marginal propensities to extraspend are zero, must also apply when they are positive. Let us assume, therefore, that all of the off-diagonal elements of M are zero. Then it can easily be shown that, as is to be expected:

(7.16)

$$
(I - M^t)(I - M)^{-1} =
\begin{bmatrix}
\dfrac{1 - {}_1E'_1{}^t}{1 - {}_1E'_1{}^t} & 0 & \cdots & 0 \\[2ex]
0 & \dfrac{1 - {}_2E'_2{}^t}{1 - {}_2E'_2{}^t} & \cdots & 0 \\[2ex]
& & \cdot & \\
& & \cdot\, \dfrac{1 - {}_nE'_n{}^t}{1 - {}_nE'_n} & \\[2ex]
0 & 0 & \cdots &
\end{bmatrix}
$$

that is, each sector's closed system multiplier is entered in the principal diagonal. Now each of these closed system multipliers approaches the minimum stable value of $1/2$;[6] consequently the multiplier for the whole economy approaches the same value as a minimum. Therefore, as long as marginal propensities to extraspend are not negative, and the economy is stable, the multiplier must not only be positive, but it must exceed the value $1/2$.

---

[6] As ${}_iE'_i$ approaches -1, $\lim\limits_{t \to \infty} (1 - {}_iE'_i{}^t)/(1 - {}_iE'_i)$ approaches the value $\frac{1}{2}$; since stability requires that ${}_iE'_i > -1$, $\frac{1}{2}$ is the minimum value. If negative marginal propensities to intraspend are ruled out, the minimum value of the multiplier is 1.

(7.16) also tells us that stability requires that *each* $_iE'_i$ be less than unity in absolute value. Now, if marginal propensities to extraspend are positive, the multiplier will be larger, and this stability condition will be reinforced. Thus we arrive at the important proposition that, not only must the average of all sectors' marginal propensity to intraspend, tr M/n, be less than unity, but, *provided every single sector's marginal propensity to extraspend is nonnegative, every single sector's marginal propensity to intraspend must be less than unity*. In mathematical terms this means that if the characteristic roots of a matrix are less than unity, and if the off-diagonal elements of the matrix are zero or positive, then each diagonal term must be less than unity. In terms of the matrix $I — M$, if each off-diagonal term is nonpositive, each diagonal term must be positive.

We may therefore draw from this section the following conclusions:

(1) A necessary condition for stability is that the sum of the marginal propensities to intraspend must be less in absolute value than the number of sectors.

(2) A necessary condition for stability of the static multiplier is that its determinant be positive.

(3) If all autonomous disbursement is of the same sign, and if there are no negative marginal propensities to extraspend, the multi-sector multiplier must exceed 1/2 in value.

(4) If there are no negative marginal propensities to extraspend, a necessary condition for stability is that each sector's marginal propensity to intraspend be less than unity.

II. THE NECESSARY AND SUFFICIENT CONDITIONS FOR STABILITY

The necessary and sufficient conditions for the stability of the system of difference equations (6.6) and (6.10) are that the roots of the characteristic polynomial (6.46) lie within the unit circle of the complex plane.[7] We shall set forth in

---

[7] We shall not consider here the peculiar case mentioned at the end of Section IV, in which roots which are not within the unit circle may be annihilated by zero coefficients. In this rare and unlikely case, the necessary and sufficient

the present section the necessary and sufficient conditions, which may be called the Schur conditions, that the roots of a polynomial lie within the unit circle. First, it will be convenient to summarize the development of necessary and sufficient stability conditions in the mathematical literature.[8]

The stability of a system of differential equations requires that the roots of its characteristic polynomial have all their real parts negative.[9] The necessary and sufficient conditions that the roots of a polynomial lie in the negative half of the complex plane were first developed by Routh.[10] Later they were derived independently by Hurwitz[11] in a more convenient determinantal form. More recently, Frazer and Duncan,[12] unaware of Hurwitz's work, reformulated the Routh conditions in the Hurwitz form.[13]

The necessary and sufficient conditions that the roots of a polynomial lie within the unit circle of the complex plane were first derived by Schur[14] and Cohn.[15] It was subsequently shown

conditions that the characteristic roots be less than unity in absolute value are not necessary conditions for stability; the further condition—the non-vanishing of the coefficients of the roots—must then be added in order to make the stability conditions necessary and sufficient.

[8] I am indebted to Professor Aurel Wintner, Professor of Mathematics at The Johns Hopkins University, for the references, given below, to the articles of Hurwitz, Cohn, and Herglotz.

[9] The solution of a system of differential equations is in terms of functions of the form $e^{\omega t}$, where ω is a complex root of the form $\mu + \nu i$. By Taylor's theorem, $e^{\omega t} = e^{\mu t}(\cos \nu t + i \sin \nu t)$; convergence therefore requires that $\mu < 0$. In the case of difference equations the solution is in terms of functions of the form λ^t, where $\lambda = e^{\omega}$, $|\lambda| = e^{\mu}$, and $\arg \lambda = \nu$. Hence, the condition $\mu < 0$ is the same as the condition $|\lambda| < 1$.

[10] E. J. Routh, *A Treatise on the Stability of a Given State of Motion*, Adams Prize Essay (London) chs. II and III; also, *Advanced Rigid Dynamics* (4th ed., London), ch. VI, §§ 290-307.

[11] A. Hurwitz, "Ueber die Bedingungen, unter welchen eine Gleichung nur Wurzeln mit negativen reellen Theilen besitzt," *Mathematische Annalen*, Vol. 46 (1895), pp. 273-284.

[12] R. A. Fraser and W. J. Duncan, "On the Criteria for the Stability of Small Motions," *Proceedings of the Royal Society of London* (Series A), Vol. 124 (1929), pp. 642-654.

[13] A statement of the Hurwitz conditions may be found in Samuelson, *Foundations of Economic Analysis*, pp. 433-434.

[14] J. Schur, "Über Potenzreihen, die im Innern des Einheitskreis beschränkt sind," *Journal für Mathematik*, Vol. 147 (1917), pp. 205-232.

[15] A. Cohn, "Über die Anzahl der Wurzeln einer algebraischen Gleichung in einem Kreise," *Mathematische Zeitschrift*, Vol. 14 (1922), pp. 110-148.

by Herglotz [16] that the Cohn conditions are equivalent to the Hurwitz conditions. The one may be transformed into the other by means of a transformation given by Schur.[17] The same transformation was in recent years used by Professor Samuelson [18] (who was unaware of the work of Schur, Cohn, and Herglotz) to derive, from the Routh-Hurwitz conditions, the necessary and sufficient conditions that the roots of a polynomial lie within the unit circle.

The Schur conditions are as follows: [19] *The necessary and sufficient conditions that the roots of the polynomial*

$$(7.17) \qquad f(\lambda) = a_0\lambda^n + a_1\lambda^{n-1} + \cdots + a_{n-1}\lambda + a_n$$

lie within the unit circle of the complex plane are that the n determinants

$$(7.18) \qquad \delta_i = \begin{vmatrix} a_0 & 0 & \cdots & 0 & a_n & a_{n-1} & \cdots & a_{n-i\,1} \\ a_1 & a_0 & \cdots & 0 & 0 & a_n & \cdots & a_{n-i\,2} \\ \cdot & \cdot & \cdot & \cdot & \cdot & \cdot & & \cdot \\ a_{i-1} & a_{i-2} & \cdots & a_0 & 0 & 0 & \cdots & a_n \\ \hline a_n & 0 & \cdots & 0 & a_0 & a_1 & \cdots & a_{i-1} \\ a_{n-1} & a_n & \cdots & 0 & 0 & a_0 & \cdots & a_{i-2} \\ \cdot & \cdot & \cdot & \cdot & \cdot & \cdot & & \cdot \\ a_{n-i\,1} & a_{n-i\,2} & \cdots & a_n & 0 & 0 & \cdots & a_0 \end{vmatrix}$$

$$(i = 1, 2, \cdots, n)$$

be all positive definite.[20] These conditions may readily be applied to the characteristic polynomial (6.46), by making the substitution $a_i = (-1)^i D_i$, where $a_0 = 1$.

---

[16] G. Herglotz, "Über die Wurzelanzahl algebraischer Gleichungen innerhalb und auf dem Einheitskreis," *Mathematische Zeitschrift*, Vol. 19 (1924), pp. 26-34.

[17] Schur, p. 228.

[18] P. A. Samuelson, "Conditions that the Roots of a Polynomial be less than Unity in Absolute Value," *Annals of Mathematical Statistics*, Vol. 12 (1941), pp. 360-364.

[19] Cf. Cohn, p. 125.

[20] In the original formulation, the coefficients of the polynomial are taken as complex; hence the two bottom partitioned matrices of δ_i are, in the complex case, not the transposes of the diagonally opposite partitioned matrices (as shown above), but the transposes of their complex conjugates. This more general case obviously does not concern us here.

It should be noted that a_0 in (7.17) is taken to be positive. It may, indeed, be taken as equal to unity without loss of generality.

Since the Schur conditions do not require any transformations, but may be derived directly from the coefficients of the characteristic polynomial, they are in a more convenient form than the Samuelson conditions.[21]

III. The Simple Aggregative Multiplier

1. We saw in Part I that simple aggregative multiplier analysis isolates Households by assuming that Business has a unit marginal propensity eventually to spend to Households, and that other sectors have a zero marginal propensity eventually to spend to Households; and furthermore, that simple aggregative dynamic multiplier analysis, as formulated by Machlup, assumes that there exists a uniform average income-propagation period. We shall now continue to make these assumptions, and analyze the interrelationships among the subdivisions of Households.

Let Households be divided into n sub-sectors, the sub-sectors being individual households or individuals, or groups of households and individuals such as countries, regions, or classes. This system is described by the system of difference equations (6.6). The sum of all these equations gives us national income (or world income, in the case of countries):

$$(7.19) \qquad \sum_{i=1}^{n} dY_i(t) = \sum_{i=1}^{n} dE_i + \sum_{j=1}^{n} \sum_{i=1}^{n} {}_j E'_i \, dY_j(t-1).$$

Likewise, the sum of equations (6.10) gives us the total income multiplier:

$$(7.20) \qquad \sum_{i=1}^{n} k_i(t) = \sum_{i=1}^{n} e_i + \sum_{j=1}^{n} \sum_{i=1}^{n} {}_j E'_i \, k_j(t-1).$$

---

[21] Dr. C. D. Long has made the objection that the above stability conditions should be translated into economic conditions. Unfortunately this is not possible. The above conditions are designed to apply to a system which we do not otherwise know to be stable or unstable. For instance, a system satisfies a necessary condition for stability if all marginal propensities to intraspend are less than unity in absolute value. But if some marginal propensities to spend (i. e., the column sums of the matrix) are greater than unity, we still do not know whether the system is stable or not. The above formula tells us what combination of marginal propensities to spend will insure stability; if any one parameter should increase, the whole system might become unstable. This is the only economic interpretation that can be made of the necessary and sufficient conditions.

Now the Keynesian assumptions imply that all income-recipients have the same marginal propensity to consume, that is, that every $\sum_{i=1}^{n} {}_jE'_i$ is the same for every j. Let every $\sum_{i=1}^{n} {}_jE'_i = c$, where c is the marginal propensity to consume. Then (7.20) reduces to the simple difference equation

$$(7.21) \qquad \sum_{i=1}^{n} k_i(t) = \sum_{i=1}^{n} e_i + c \sum_{i=1}^{n} k_i(t-1)$$

whose solution is

$$(7.22) \qquad \sum_{i=1}^{n} k_i(t) = \frac{1}{1-c} (1-c^t) \sum_{i=1}^{n} e_i.$$

Thus when the autonomous expenditure takes the form of an autonomous redistribution of income (so that $\sum_{i=1}^{n} e_i = 0$), the multiplier is zero; and when the autonomous expenditure is a net change in expenditure in one direction, so that $\sum_{i=1}^{n} e_i = 1$, the multiplier is the familiar

$$(7.23) \qquad \sum_{i=1}^{n} k_i(t) = \frac{1-c^t}{1-c},$$

which reduces to $\frac{1}{1-c}$ as $t \to \infty$ if $|c| < 1$.

2. The above derivation may be formalized into the following theorem:

THEOREM 4. *If all sectors' marginal propensities to spend are equal to one another, the multi-sector multiplier reduces to the simple aggregative multiplier formula.*

PROOF. Let each sector's marginal propensity to spend, $\sum_{i=1}^{n} {}_jE'_i$ (that is, each column sum of M), be equal to c. Then

$$(7.24) \quad (1, 1, \cdots, 1)M = (c, c, \cdots, c)$$

and

$$(7.25) \quad (1, 1, \cdots, 1)M^2 = (c, c, \cdots, c)M = (c^2, c^2, \cdots, c^2).$$

Thus it is seen that

(7. 26) $\qquad (1, 1, \cdots, 1) M^t = (c^t, c^t, \cdots, c^t).$

Now it follows directly from (6. 17) that

(7. 27) $\qquad (I - M^t) e = (I - M) k(t).$

Since each column sum of $I - M$ is equal to $1 - c$, and since, from (7.26), each column sum of $I - M^t$ is equal to $1 - c^t$, the column sums of the vectors (7.27) are

(7. 28) $\qquad (1 - c^t) \sum_{i=1}^{n} e_i = (1 - c) \sum_{i=1}^{n} k_i(t),$

so that

(7. 22) $\qquad \sum_{i=1}^{n} k_i(t) = \frac{1}{1 - c} (1 - c^t) \sum_{i=1}^{n} e_i$

as before.

3. (7.22) corresponds to the scalar solution (6.59), where $s = n$ and

(7. 29) $\qquad \sum_{i=1}^{n} \bar{k}_i = \sum_{i=1}^{n} \Delta'_i / \Delta = \frac{1}{1 - c}.$

From (7. 22) and (7. 29) we know that

(7. 30) $\qquad \dfrac{\sum_{i=1}^{n} k_i(t)}{\sum_{i=1}^{n} \bar{k}_i} - 1 = - c^t.$

Consequently, equation (6.69) becomes

(7. 31) $\qquad \begin{bmatrix} 1 & 1 & 1 & \cdots & 1 \\ \lambda_1 & \lambda_2 & \lambda_3 & \cdots & \lambda_n \\ \lambda_1^2 & \lambda_2^2 & \lambda_3^2 & \cdots & \lambda_n^2 \\ \cdot & \cdot & \cdot & \cdots & \cdot \\ \lambda_1^{n-1} & \lambda_2^{n-1} & \lambda_3^{n-1} & \cdots & \lambda_n^{n-1} \end{bmatrix} \begin{bmatrix} K_1 \\ K_2 \\ K_3 \\ \cdot \\ K_n \end{bmatrix} = \begin{bmatrix} -1 \\ -c \\ -c^2 \\ \cdot \\ -c^{n-1} \end{bmatrix}.$

We know from (7. 22) that c satisfies our system of equations, so that one of the roots—say λ_s—must be equal to c. Hence the time-path vector of (7. 31) is equal to the s-th column vector of the Vandermonde matrix, with sign changed. By (6. 72), the value of the j-th constant—K_j—in the vector of constants is equal to the j-th-column Cramer determinant of the Vandermonde matrix.[22] Thus the s-th-column Cramer determinant will be simply the negative of the Vandermonde determinant,[23] and all the other Cramer determinants will vanish because they will contain two linearly dependent column vectors. The s-th constant—K_s—is therefore equal to minus unity, and all the other constants vanish. Thus, in the Keynesian case, one of the roots is equal to the marginal propensity to consume, and all the other roots are annihilated.

IV. THE CONDITIONS FOR OSCILLATORY BEHAVIOR

1. So far in this chapter we have been chiefly concerned with equilibrium and the stability of equilibrium. We have been occupied with the characteristic values of the equilibrium solution of the system, and with the conditions under which the dynamic system converges to the equilibrium of the static system. We may now examine the properties of the path along which the system moves after it has been disturbed from an initial state of equilibrium.

The time-path of the flow of receipts may be of two sorts: monotonic and non-monotonic. A *monotonic* time-path is one which is either continually rising or continually falling whereas a *non-monotonic* time-path is one which contains one or more "waves," whereby a fall is followed by a rise or a rise is followed by a fall. An oscillatory time-path is one which is characterized by a regular succession of waves, by recurrent ups and downs. These various time-paths are illustrated in Figure 12.

In the case of the simple aggregative multiplier, as is well-known, the flow of income must be monotonic, unless the marginal propensity to spend is negative. This is no longer necessarily the case, however, with the multi-sector multiplier. It has been shown by Machlup that a change in the exports of one country to another may bring about a "wave" in one

---

[22] We use the expression i-th column Cramer determinant to mean the determinant of the matrix formed by replacing the i-th column of the Vandermonde matrix by the time-path vector.

[23] The Vandermonde determinant is equal to $\prod_{i>j} (\lambda_i - \lambda_j)$.

country's income.[24] An autonomous increase in exports will have the initial effect of increasing a country's income; if the other country's marginal propensity to spend is higher than that of the exporting country, the contraction of income in

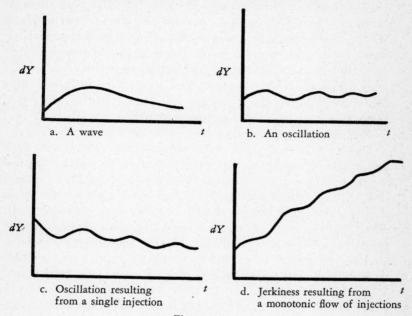

a. A wave   b. An oscillation

c. Oscillation resulting   d. Jerkiness resulting from
from a single injection   a monotonic flow of injections

Figure 12.

the importing country will soon be great enough to reduce the income of the exporting country relative to the level to which it first rose because of the exports.[25]

Recently the claim was made by Goodwin that the time-path of the multi-sector multiplier was necessarily an oscillatory one; "not only," he stated, "may this system exhibit oscillatory behavior—it must do so." [26] Owing to objections which I made to Goodwin's analysis, this claim was later retracted.[27]

[24] Cf. Machlup, *International Trade and the National Income Multiplier*, pp. 66-84, 160-169.

[25] *Ibid.*, p. 83.

[26] Goodwin, "The Multiplier as Matrix," p. 550.

[27] Cf. J. S. Chipman, "Professor Goodwin's Matrix Multiplier," and R. M. Goodwin, "Does the Matrix Multiplier Oscillate?" *Economic Journal*, LX, (December, 1950), pp. 753-763, 764-770.

The basis for Goodwin's original claim lay in his assumption with regard to the marginal propensities to intraspend. It is always possible to divide the economy into units small enough (such as individuals and firms) for each to have a zero marginal propensity to intraspend. In such a model, the trace of the multiplier matrix is equal to zero. As we saw in Section I of this chapter, the trace of a matrix is equal to the sum of its latent roots; consequently if the trace is zero, the sum of the roots is zero, and since some roots will have positive real parts, some others must have negative real parts. Goodwin was thus able to prove that the roots cannot all be positive and real. From this he drew the conclusion that the time-path of the multiplier process must of necessity be oscillatory.

The existence of roots with negative real parts does not, however, necessitate oscillatory behavior; it provides only for the *possibility* of oscillatory behavior. Only if it could be shown that all the roots have negative real parts (which we know is not the case) or that roots with negative real parts dominate the remaining roots, would it follow that the time-path of the multiplier process was oscillatory. In the following paragraphs we shall examine the extent to which oscillatory or wavelike motion in the multiplier process may be expected to take place.

2. There are three factors which determine whether or not the time-path of the multiplier process is monotonic. These are (1) the signs of the parameters (the participants' marginal propensities to spend to themselves and to one another), (2) the signs of the autonomous injections of disbursements into the economy, and (3) the time-path of these autonomous disbursements.

From an examination of the aggregative multiplier formula, it is clear that a negative marginal propensity to spend would bring about an oscillatory time-path in the multiplier process. Any negative elements in the marginal propensities to spend in a multi-sector economy may therefore be expected to produce a tendency towards oscillatory behavior in the sector's receipts. A necessary condition for the monotonic behavior of sector receipts would appear to be that all the elements in the multiplier matrix be nonnegative.

As we saw above, it was found by Machlup that the transfer of disbursements from one sector to another may bring about a wave in a sector's receipts. In fact it is possible to construct simple examples in which such a shift in disbursements will give rise to *oscillations* in sector receipts.[28] No such waves or oscillations occur, however (barring negative propensities), when the multiplicand is a change in disbursements *in the same direction* for every sector of the economy. A second necessary condition for monotonic behavior appears, then, to be that all autonomous disbursements must be of the same sign.

The third factor which influences the time-path of sector receipts is, of course, the time-path of autonomous disbursements. Clearly, if autonomous disbursements fluctuate from period to period, one may expect fluctuations to appear in sector receipts; does it follow, conversely, that a monotonic flow of disbursements will give rise to a monotonic flow of receipts?

At this point we may digress to consider two kinds of multiplier concepts that are employed in the economic literature. One of these may be called the "constant-injections" or "continuous-impulse" multiplier or, in Samuelson's words, the "steady-plateau multiplier." It tells us the rate of receipts (for any sector) resulting from the disturbance of an original equilibrium position by a steady stream, or plateau, of autonomous injections. It is also the same as the *cumulated* change in the rate of receipts resulting from a single unrepeated dose of injections.[29] The second of these multipliers is the "single-injection multiplier" or, in Samuelson's terminology, the

---

[28] Take the example of the following matrix:

$$\begin{pmatrix} 0 & a \\ b & 0 \end{pmatrix}$$

Let us assume that there is an autonomous change in the level of sector's 1's "exports" to sector 2. Then by (6.13) we have the series

$$\begin{pmatrix} dY_1 \\ dY_2 \end{pmatrix} = \begin{pmatrix} 1 & 0 \\ 0 & 1 \end{pmatrix}\begin{pmatrix} 1 \\ -1 \end{pmatrix} + \begin{pmatrix} 0 & a \\ b & 0 \end{pmatrix}\begin{pmatrix} 1 \\ -1 \end{pmatrix} + \begin{pmatrix} ab & 0 \\ 0 & ab \end{pmatrix}\begin{pmatrix} 1 \\ -1 \end{pmatrix}$$

$$+ \begin{pmatrix} 0 & ab^2 \\ a^2b & 0 \end{pmatrix}\begin{pmatrix} 1 \\ -1 \end{pmatrix} + \cdots$$

$$= \begin{pmatrix} 1 \\ -1 \end{pmatrix} + \begin{pmatrix} -a \\ b \end{pmatrix} + \begin{pmatrix} ab \\ -ab \end{pmatrix} + \begin{pmatrix} -a^2b \\ ab^2 \end{pmatrix} + \begin{pmatrix} a^2b^2 \\ -a^2b^2 \end{pmatrix} + \cdots.$$

[29] The identity of the "horizontal" and "cumulated" multipliers was proved by Samuelson in "A Fundamental Multiplier Identity," pp. 221-226. See also Lange, "The Theory of the Multiplier," pp. 244-245.

"single-impulse" or "unit-pulse" multiplier. It tells us the rate of sector receipts at any time resulting from the disturbance of the economy from equilibrium by a single unrepeated vector of injections.

The continuous-impulse multiplier is represented by the expression $(I - M^t)(I - M)^{-1}$ which, by (6.15), expands to the *series* $I + M + M^2 + \cdots$. The single-impulse multiplier, on the other hand,[30] is represented by the expression M^t, which gives rise to the *sequence* $I, M, M^2, \cdots$. The single-impulse multiplier sequence is simply the first difference of the continuous-impulse multiplier series. If the sequence contains no negative elements, the series cannot oscillate; for the series to oscillate, the sequence must not only oscillate, but alternate in sign as well.

In the general case, there is neither a single injection at one point of time, nor a steady stream of constant injections, but rather there is an injections vector whose time-shape is of undefined form. Of special interest to us is an injections vector whose time shape is monotonic.[31] If we start from zero initial conditions (which implies no restriction, for receipts are measured in deviations from initial values), we may assume that the vector of injections, from that time on, is monotonically changing with time. The constant-injections multiplier is the limiting case of this monotonic-injections multiplier, for it is the case in which injections remain unchanged over time after the initial change has taken place; it is the case, so to speak, in which we do not keep climbing a mountain, but climb one cliff and thereafter proceed along a plateau. But a mountain may be considered as a succession of plateaux, superimposed one upon the other. In order to obtain the monotonic-injections multiplier, we need simply add a new constant-injections multiplier in every period to the previous one; the constant-injections vector corresponding to the new constant-injections multiplier is equal simply to the difference between the new level of

[30] Samuelson, "A Fundamental Multiplier Identity," p. 224.

[31] This excludes the important case mentioned by Professor Goodwin (the "Slutsky effect") in which the injections vector contains random fluctuations over time. Cf. R. M. Goodwin, "Does the Matrix Multiplier Oscillate?" p. 770. If the single-injection multiplier oscillates, then it is certainly true that the random-injections multiplier will do so as well.

injections and the level in the previous period. If the constant-injections multiplier is monotonic, then the monotonic-injections multiplier must be monotonic as well, since the latter is obtained by the addition of constant-injections multipliers.

We now come to the following simple, though fundamental, theorem:

THEOREM 5. *If there are no negative elements in the marginal propensities to spend, and if autonomous disbursements are of the same sign in every sector of the economy, the monotonic-injections multiplier is monotonic.*

PROOF. If the constant-injections multiplier is monotonic, we know that the monotonic-injections multiplier is also monotonic. We are therefore to prove that the series

$$dY(t) = (I - M^t)(I - M)^{-1} = (I + M + M^2 + \cdots)dE$$

is monotonic provided that (1) the elements of M are all non-negative and (2) the elements of dE are all either nonnegative or nonpositive. The proof is trivial: powers of matrices whose elements are all nonnegative cannot contain negative elements; hence the series $I + M + M^2 + \cdots$ is monotonic. Since the elements of dE are all ≥ 0 or ≤ 0, the series $(I + M + M^2 + \cdots)dE$ is also monotonic.

3. It is an interesting fact that a system may be set up which necessarily has characteristic roots with negative real parts, and which nevertheless is necessarily non-oscillatory. Evidently there must be an automatic tendency in such a system for these roots to be constrained.

Consider the special case discussed in the previous section, in which (*vide* (31)) the time-path vector turned out to be none other than the simple multiplier progression, with sign changed. In such a system, we saw that if the s-th column of the Vandermonde matrix was the negative of the time-path vector, the s-th arbitrary constant was equal to -1, and the other constants vanished. This system may also describe an economy in which non-Household sectors are explicitly included. Let us therefore consider a system in which all sectors but Finance are included, and in which transaction periods are of uniform duration. Let us assume that all organisms' marginal propensities to spend are the same, so that firms' and governments' marginal propensities to spend are equal to households' marginal propensities to consume and pay taxes.[32]

In such an economy, the s-th root is again equal to the uniform propensity to spend, and is completely dominant, whilst the remaining roots are annihilated. The path of total transactions is monotonic, just as in the case of the previous section the path of total income was monotonic. And, it should be noted, this holds true even in the case of the single-impulse multiplier. Complex and negative roots are all annihilated; even if there should be only one positive real root, that root would completely dominate the solution.

Suppose, now, that the marginal propensities to spend of the various sectors of the economy are *nearly* equal to one another. It is clear intuitively that in this case the time-path vector of (6.69) will be very nearly the same as that in (7.13), and may therefore be written $\{-1, -c_1, -c_2{}^2, \cdots, -c_{n-1}^{n-1}\}$, where c_t is a weighted marginal propensity to spend which varies with time because of the change in the weights applied to each sector's marginal propensity to spend as receipts change. It is clear also that, in this case, the time-path vector may be approximated by the negative of the s-th column vector of the Vandermonde matrix, written $\{1, \lambda_s, \lambda_s{}^2, \cdots, \lambda_s{}^{n-1}\}$, where λ_s is a mean value of the varying aggregate marginal propensity to spend, $c_1, c_2, \cdots, c_{n-1}$. The matrix formed by substituting the time-path vector in the s-th column of the Vandermonde matrix will therefore be nearly the same as the Vandermonde matrix itself; consequently the matrix formed by substituting the time-path vector in any column but the s-th of the Vandermonde matrix, will make the latter nearly singular. It follows that the s-th arbitrary constant will be nearly -1, and that the remaining constants will be nearly zero. The s-th root is then a weighted average marginal propensity to spend, and the changes in the average marginal propensity to spend through time are accounted for by the presence of the other roots as

[32] If governments have zero marginal propensities to spend, we may exclude them from the model, and assume that firms' marginal propensities to spend are all equal to the uniform marginal propensity to consume.

correction factors. As marginal propensities to spend diverge more and more, the s-th root becomes less and less dominant, and the others become more and more influential.

To what extent may the several marginal propensities diverge before oscillations set in? It appears that, as long as there are no negative elements in the marginal propensities to spend, and no greater than unit marginal propensities to spend, oscillations in total transactions will never set in as a result of a single injection.

Consider the case in which $M = \begin{pmatrix} 0 & .9 \\ .1 & 0 \end{pmatrix}$. The unit-pulse multiplier for this matrix is

(7. 32)

$$\begin{pmatrix} 1 & 0 \\ 0 & 1 \end{pmatrix}, \begin{pmatrix} 0 & .9 \\ .1 & 0 \end{pmatrix}, \begin{pmatrix} .09 & 0 \\ 0 & .09 \end{pmatrix}, \begin{pmatrix} 0 & .081 \\ .009 & 0 \end{pmatrix}, \begin{pmatrix} .0081 & 0 \\ 0 & .0081 \end{pmatrix}, \cdots$$

While there is oscillation in the sense that the money flow passes back and forth from one sector to the other, period by period, there is no oscillation in total transactions, for the column sums of (7. 32) form the vector progression

(7. 33) $(1, 1), (.1, .9), (.09, .09), (.009, .081), (.0081, .0081), \cdots$

which is monotonically decreasing. Consider, on the other hand, the case in which $M = \begin{pmatrix} 0 & 1.1 \\ .1 & 0 \end{pmatrix}$. Here the unit-pulse matrix expansion is

(7. 34)

$$\begin{pmatrix} 1 & 0 \\ 0 & 1 \end{pmatrix}, \begin{pmatrix} 0 & 1.1 \\ .1 & 0 \end{pmatrix}, \begin{pmatrix} .11 & 0 \\ 0 & .11 \end{pmatrix}, \begin{pmatrix} 0 & .121 \\ .011 & 0 \end{pmatrix}, \begin{pmatrix} .0121 & 0 \\ 0 & .0121 \end{pmatrix}, \cdots$$

which gives us oscillations in total transactions, for the column-sum vector progression is

(7. 35) $(1, 1), (.1, 1.1), (.11, .11), (.111, .121), (.0121, .0121), \cdots$

Our conjecture is verified by the following theorem:

THEOREM 6. *Let M be an $n \times n$ matrix satisfying the following two conditions: (a) M contains no negative elements; (b) the column sums of M are either all ≤ 1 or all ≥ 1. Then the sequence*

(7. 36) $(1, 1, \cdots, 1)M^t$ $(t = 0, 1, 2, \cdots)$

is a monotonic one.

Proof. First let the column sums of M be all less than or equal to unity, that is,

(7. 37) $(1, 1, \cdots, 1)M \leq (1, 1, \cdots, 1)$.

Since M contains no negative elements, we may multiply both sides of (7.37) by M successively, obtaining

(7. 38)

$(1, 1, \cdots, 1)M^2 \leq (1, 1, \cdots, 1)M \leq (1, 1, \cdots, 1)$

$(1, 1, \cdots, 1)M^3 \leq (1, 1, \cdots, 1)M^2 \leq (1, 1, \cdots, 1)M \leq (1, 1, \cdots, 1)$

$\cdot \quad \cdot \quad \cdot \quad \cdot \quad \cdot \quad \cdot \quad \cdot \quad \cdot \quad \cdot \quad \cdot \quad \cdot \quad \cdot \quad \cdot \quad \cdot \quad \cdot \quad \cdot$

$(1, 1, \cdots, 1)M^t \leq (1, 1, \cdots, 1)M^{t-1} \leq \cdots \leq (1, 1, \cdots, 1)$,

which proves that the sequence (7.36) is a monotonically decreasing one. Similarly, if the column sums of M are all greater than or equal to unity, so that

(7. 39) $(1, 1, \cdots, 1)M \geq (1, 1, \cdots, 1)$,

it follows that

(7. 40) $(1, 1, \cdots, 1)M^t \geq (1, 1, \cdots, 1)M^{t-1} \geq \cdots \geq (1, 1, \cdots, 1)$,

so that the sequence (7.36) is montonically increasing.

Thus if all sectors have less than unit marginal propensities to spend, or if they all have greater than unit marginal propensities to spend, the single-impulse multiplier for total transactions will be monotonic; whereas if some sectors have less than unit marginal propensities to spend while others have greater than unit marginal propensities to spend, oscillations may arise in total transactions. Such oscillations will arise because the weighted average marginal propensity to spend will fluctuate as the money flow passes from sectors with less than unit marginal propensities to spend to sectors with greater than unit marginal propensities to spend. But if marginal propensities to spend are either all less than or equal to unity, or all greater than or equal to unity, total transactions will be monotonic, and only the distribution of these transactions may be oscillatory.

In identifying the total receipts of all participants in the model with transactions, we have left out non-transactors such as financial institutions and our fictitious goblins or collecting agencies. If goblins as well as genuine transactors are included in the model, indicating the existence of unequal transaction periods, the receipts of the former must not be included in the summation.[33] The sector of genuine transactors must then be thought of as an open economy trading with imaginary transactors; since the genuine transactors form only a part of the economy, their receipts will be subject to fluctuations as a result of a single impulse of injections, even if the marginal propensities to spend of all sectors are either all less than or equal to unity or greater than or equal to unity. In exactly the same way, fluctuations in Household receipts (income) may take place after a single impulse, since the money flow, as it passes back and forth among the participants, circulates unevenly through the hands of any single participant or group of participants. The existence of unequal transaction periods contributes to oscillatory behavior since it causes the money flow to be withdrawn from actual participation in an uneven way as it passes through the hands of sectors with varying transaction periods.

Suppose now that there are no negative parameters, and that all sectors' marginal propensities to spend are less than or equal to unity (or greater than or equal to unity). Then if transaction periods are equal, there will be no collecting agenices in the model, and there can be no oscillation in total transactions resulting from a single injection. Likewise if income periods are equal, there will be no firms or govenments in the model, and there can be no oscillation in total income resulting from a single injection. To assume equal transaction periods is to assume away the existence of this type of oscillatory motion in total transactions, and to assume equal income periods is to assume away the existence of such oscillatory motion in total income.

---

[33] No real harm to our insight into the economic process would result, it must be confessed, if goblins' incomes were included in total transactions, just as no harm would result if the services of housewives were included in national income.

It is a very interesting fact, as borne out by our analysis as well as by that of Goodwin, that the greater the divergence among the disbursement functions of the various sectors of the economy (divergence, that is to say, among sectors' marginal propensities to spend and among the length of sectors' transaction periods), the greater is the tendency towards oscillatory behavior of their transactions as the result of a single injection of disbursements, and towards a jerky behavior of their transactions as the result of monotonic injections of disbursements. The greater the heterogeneity of the sectors of the economy, the more fluctuating is the behavior of the economy as a whole. This is perhaps the best illustration of the dangers inherent in exclusively aggregative economic analysis.

4. We have found that under the assumption that there are no negative marginal propensities to spend and no autonomous injections of opposite sign (i. e. exports or transfers), there can be no oscillation in any sector's receipts issuing from a monotonic flow of autonomous injections, but at the most, a wavelike jerkiness as shown in Figure 12d. We also saw that if the sectors' marginal propensities to spend were either *all* less than or equal to one or *all* greater than or equal to one, there could be no oscillations in total receipts (including the receipts of the fictitious collecting agencies) as the result of a single injection. In other words, there can be no oscillation in total transactions if transaction periods are equal, and no oscillation in total income if income periods are equal. It still remains to determine to what extent a single injection may give rise to oscillations in transactions, income, and individual sector receipts, in the general case.

Let us take a simple example in which all sectors but those in the Business and Households spheres are assumed to have zero marginal propensities to spend, and in which the Business and Households divisions are taken as homogeneous sectors. It will be assumed that Business and Households have zero marginal propensities to intraspend, that Households' marginal propensity to spend to Business (the marginal propensity to consume) is equal to c, and that Business' marginal propensity to spend to Households is equal to unity (Say's Law). Then, assuming that the autonomous disbursement all goes to Households, we have the matrix expansion

(7. 41) $$\begin{pmatrix} k_H(t) \\ k_B(t) \end{pmatrix} = \Big[\begin{pmatrix} 1 & 0 \\ 0 & 1 \end{pmatrix} + \begin{pmatrix} 0 & 1 \\ c & 0 \end{pmatrix} + \begin{pmatrix} c & 0 \\ 0 & c \end{pmatrix}$$
$$+ \begin{pmatrix} 0 & c \\ c^2 & 0 \end{pmatrix} + \begin{pmatrix} c & 0 \\ 0 & c^2 \end{pmatrix} + \cdots \Big] \begin{pmatrix} 1 \\ 0 \end{pmatrix}$$

which gives us, for the national income multiplier,

(7. 42) $$k_H(t) = 1 + 0 + c + 0 + c^2 + \cdots.$$

Now if we choose to analyze this process in terms of the income period (which in this case is precisely equal to the sum of Households' and Business' transaction periods, equal, that is to say, to the sum of the lag between Households' receipts and disbursements to Business and the lag between Business' receipts and disbursements to Households) we obtain the equivalent series:

(7. 43) $$k_H(t) = 1 + c + c^2 + \cdots.$$

In the first case there is a jerky movement, and in the second there is none; yet these two progressions are equivalent. Whether or not jerkiness appears depends upon the definition of the time lag. In this model, Households receive income in discrete payments made regularly in intervals of income periods. The jerkiness in income that appears in the transaction-period analysis is merely a reflection of the fact that payments to Households are made in intervals of income periods rather than made continuously over the duration of the interval.

The assumption in the above example that Business has a zero marginal propensity to intraspend implies complete vertical integration of industry. It is therefore a most unrealistic assumption. Let us examine the properties of a system described by the matrix $M = \begin{pmatrix} .1 & .3 \\ .7 & .7 \end{pmatrix}$, in which the marginal propensity to consume of .8 is partly (to the amount of .1) devoted to intra-Households expenditure, and in which only .3 of Business' marginal propensity to spend of 1 accrues directly to Households—the remaining .7 being devoted to inter-firm transactions. This system has the following multiplier progression:

$$(7.44) \quad \begin{pmatrix} k_H(t) \\ k_B(t) \end{pmatrix} = \left[\begin{pmatrix} 1 & 0 \\ 0 & 1 \end{pmatrix} + \begin{pmatrix} .1 & .3 \\ .7 & .7 \end{pmatrix} + \begin{pmatrix} .22 & .24 \\ .56 & .7 \end{pmatrix} \right.$$

$$\left. + \begin{pmatrix} .19 & .234 \\ .556 & .658 \end{pmatrix} + \cdots \right] \begin{pmatrix} 1 \\ 0 \end{pmatrix}.$$

This gives us the income multiplier, in terms of transaction periods:

$$(7.45) \qquad k_H(t) = 1 + .1 + .22 + .19 + \cdots.$$

Here again we have a jerky movement in income, though the jerks are not so marked as those in (7.42).

Let us finally take a third example in which there is still less integration of industry than in the previous example. This case may be described by the matrix $M = \begin{pmatrix} .1 & .1 \\ .7 & .9 \end{pmatrix}$, where only .1 of Business' marginal propensity to spend accrues directly to Households. The multiplier progression for this system is:

$$(7.46) \quad \begin{pmatrix} k_H(t) \\ k_B(t) \end{pmatrix} = \left[\begin{pmatrix} 1 & 0 \\ 0 & 1 \end{pmatrix} + \begin{pmatrix} .1 & .1 \\ .7 & .9 \end{pmatrix} + \begin{pmatrix} .08 & .1 \\ .7 & .88 \end{pmatrix} \right.$$

$$\left. + \begin{pmatrix} .078 & .098 \\ .686 & .862 \end{pmatrix} + \begin{pmatrix} .0764 & .096 \\ .672 & .8444 \end{pmatrix} + \cdots \right] \begin{pmatrix} 1 \\ 0 \end{pmatrix}.$$

The income multiplier, in transaction periods, is therefore:

$$(7.47) \qquad k_H(t) = 1 + .1 + .08 + .078 + .0764 + \cdots.$$

In this example there is no jerkiness at all. It appears, then, that the greater is the degree of vertical integration, the greater is the tendency towards oscillatory behavior of the unit-pulse multiplier.

The above three examples may also be described in terms of larger matrices. The Households and Business sectors may be divided into their component households and firms, without changing the assumptions of the model, provided all households are assigned the same marginal propensity to spend, and all firms are likewise given equal marginal propensities to spend. In this way matrices can be set up whose diagonal elements (the marginal propensities to intraspend) are all zero, and which nevertheless show the same properties as the small matrices given in the above examples. It is therefore possible to have a completely monotonic single-impulse multiplier even when the trace of the multiplier matrix vanishes. The mere subdividing of the economy does not *itself* reveal any tendency towards oscillatory behavior of the receipts of the sectors which are subdivided. Subdivision may *in fact*, however, reveal oscillatory behavior in two ways. First, the subdivision of a sector may reveal oscillation in the *distribution* of receipts among the sub-sectors.[34] Secondly, if the sector is heterogeneous, subdivision of it into internally homogeneous groups may reveal oscillations which were hidden by the aggregation of these groups. But the subdivision itself does not change the character of the system. It is quite possible for individual sector receipts to be oscillatory, but the third example—which probably gives a better picture of the industrial economy than the second [35]—provides a fairly strong basis for the belief that the unit-impulse income multiplier in a normal industrial economy is not likely to be oscillatory.

In the third example, the positive roots are dominant. In the second example, however, neither the positive nor the negative roots are dominant. The time-path vector is oscillatory, but negative in sign throughout; any column vector in the Vandermonde matrix, on the other hand, is either monotonic (if the root is positive) or has elements alternately positive and negative (if the root is negative).[36] There is therefore no column vector in the Vandermonde matrix which is similar to the time-path vector; consequently there is no dominant root. Negative and positive roots combine together to form a wavelike, though non-oscillatory, monotonic-injections multiplier.

The factor which determines whether the multiplier is oscillatory or monotonic is not the existence or non-existence of

[34] Suppose we wish to describe a system in which two persons pass a dollar bill back and forth to each other. This system is described by the matrix

$$M = \begin{pmatrix} 0 & 1 \\ 1 & 0 \end{pmatrix}.$$

We know that a dollar is being disbursed in every period, yet the distribution of that dollar oscillates. Total receipts are constant, but each person's receipts oscillate. If we were only interested in total receipts to begin with, then the subdivision was unnecessary.

[35] I owe this opinion to Dr. C. D. Long.

[36] If the root is complex, the result will in effect be the same as if it is negative, except that the amplitude of the fluctuation will not be the same.

negative or complex roots, but rather the domination or non-domination of the solution by these roots. The existence of roots which are not real and positive is a necessary but not sufficient condition for oscillatory behavior, provided always that autonomous injections into the economy are not of opposite sign.

If autonomous transfer of disbursements is included in the multiplicand, so that the vector e contains elements of opposite sign, then the existence of negative or complex roots is not even a necessary condition for non-monotonic behavior. Even if all roots are positive and real, it is quite possible for the passage of receipts through time not to be monotonic. This is illustrated by Machlup's "waves" referred to above; the roots of the matrices corresponding to his examples are positive and real. Consequently the existence of negative or complex characteristic roots is neither a necessary nor a sufficient condition for non-monotonic behavior.

We may then ask whether the same situation holds in the case of the analysis of stability conditions. Fortunately it will be found that if the matrix has no negative elements, no characteristic root which is greater than unity can be annihilated. If the matrix elements are allowed to be of any sign, however, it is possible to devise cases in which roots which lie outside the unit circle are annihilated or virtually annihilated. For instance, any roots which do not lie within the unit circle will be respectively annihilated or virtually annihilated if the column sums of the matrix are equal or nearly equal, and less than unity, so that the flow of receipts will be stable or virtually stable.[37] In such a case, the condition that the latent roots of a matrix lie within the unit circle of the complex plane is a sufficient but not a necessary condition for stability.

---

[37] Any root which lies outside the unit circle will eventually dominate the solution provided its coefficient is not zero. But if this coefficient is extremely small, the time it takes for the root to dominate may be quite long—longer than the economically-relevant period of time under consideration. In this sense it may be said that for practical purposes the root is "virtually" annihilated. Strictly speaking, however, the case in which the root would be annihilated is so rare and unlikely that it is of purely formal interest.

CHAPTER 8

FURTHER DEVELOPMENTS AND REFINEMENTS

I. Changes in Relative Prices

Up till now we have implicitly assumed that there are no changes in relative prices and interest rates. We may now relax that assumption. The disbursements of sector i to sector j may be considered as a function not only of i's receipts, but also of the prices [1] (or price indices) of all sectors of the economy.[2]

Denoting autonomous disbursements to j by E_j, k's disbursements to j by $_kE_j$, and the price of j's product (or price index of its products) as a function of j's receipts by $p_j(Y_j)$, we may write for j's receipts equation:

$$(8.1) \quad Y_j = E_j + {_1}E_j[Y_1, p_1(Y_1), \cdots, p_n(Y_n)]$$
$$+ {_2}E_j[Y_2, p_1(Y_1), \cdots, p_n(Y_n)]$$
$$+ \cdots + {_n}E_j[Y_n, p_1(Y_1), \cdots, p_n(Y_n)].$$

Thus,

$$(8.2) \quad dY_j = dE_j + ({_1}E_{j_{Y_1}} + \sum_{k=1}^{n} {_k}E_{j_{p_1}} p'_1) dY_1$$
$$+ ({_2}E_{j_{Y_2}} + \sum_{k=1}^{n} {_k}E_{j_{p_2}} p'_2 \, dY_2)$$
$$+ \cdots + ({_n}E_{j_{Y_n}} + \sum_{k=1}^{n} {_k}E_{j_{p_n}} p'_n) dY_n.$$

That is to say, as j's receipts rise, j's price will rise, so that all sectors' disbursements to every sector will change.

If changes in disbursements lag equally behind changes in receipts and changes in prices (i. e., $_kE_j(t) = {_k}E_j[Y_k(t-1),$ $p_1(t-1), \cdots, p_n(t-1)]$) and if changes in prices follow changes in receipts instantaneously (i. e., $p_j(t) = p_j[Y_j(t)]$, then it is clear that (8.2) becomes

---

[1] This includes prices of securities and factors of production.
[2] In order to remove money illusion, one of these prices may be taken as *numéraire* and set equal to unity.

$$(8.3) \qquad dY_j(t) = dE_j + ({}_1E_{j_{Y_1}} + \sum_{k=1}^{n} {}_kE_{j_{p_1}} \, p'_1) \, dY_1(t-1)$$

$$+ ({}_2E_{j_{Y_2}} + \sum_{k=1}^{n} {}_kE_{j_{p_2}} \, p'_2) \, dY_2(t-1)$$

$$+ \cdots + ({}_nE_{j_{Y_n}} + \sum_{k=1}^{n} {}_kE_{j_{p_n}} \, p'_n) \, dY_n(t-1).$$

Thus, when we take account of price changes induced by changes in receipts, i's marginal propensity to spend to j becomes

$$(8.4) \qquad {}_iE'_j = {}_iE_{j\,Y_i} + \sum_{k=1}^{n} {}_kE_{j_{p_i}} \, p'_i.$$

We form the matrices

$$(8.5) \qquad L = ({}_iE_{j_{Y_i}})$$

and

$$(8.6) \qquad K = (\sum_{k=1}^{n} {}_kE_{j_{p_i}})$$

and the column vector

$$(8.7) \qquad p' = \begin{bmatrix} p'_1 \\ p'_2 \\ \vdots \\ p'_n \end{bmatrix}$$

where the i subscript refers to columns and the j subscript to rows. The matrix M then becomes

$$(8.8) \qquad M = L + Kp'.$$

The analysis of the preceding chapters holds generally for the adjusted matrix M.

II. THE PRINCIPLE OF ACCELERATION

So far in this work we have taken no account of the "principle of acceleration." It is quite possible, however, to introduce this concept by making further refinements in the analysis. We may now briefly indicate a possible method of dealing with this phenomenon within the framework of our system.

The acceleration principle states[3] that since the quantity of fixed capital is a function of the volume of output, which (if there is no inventory accumulation or decumulation) is equivalent to the volume of sales, the rate of *investment* is a function of the *rate of change* of sales. In terms of our model, this means that a sector's purchases of capital goods from other sectors are a function of the rate of change of that sector's receipts.

For the sake of simplicity we may assume, following Samuelson,[4] that the disbursements of a given sector to others for capital goods, at time t, are a linear function of the change in that sector's receipts between time $t-2$ and $t-1$.[5] We may define sector j's acceleration coefficient for the products of sector i as follows:

$$(8.9) \qquad a_{ij} = \frac{\partial_j E_i}{\partial [Y_j(t-1) - Y_j(t-2)]} .$$

Many acceleration coefficients will, of course, be zero. If the i-th sector belongs to Households, Government, or Finance, a_{ij} will be equal to zero; such will also be the case if the i-th sector is a firm which sells services and non-durable goods. The acceleration coefficient will be different from zero only if the i-th sector is one that disposes of durable goods. Consequently, the acceleration matrix,

$$(8.10) \qquad A = \begin{bmatrix} a_{11} & a_{12} \cdot \cdot \cdot a_{1n} \\ a_{21} & a_{22} \cdot \cdot \cdot a_{2n} \\ \cdot & \cdot \quad \cdot \quad \cdot \\ a_{n1} & a_{n2} \cdot \cdot \cdot a_{nn} \end{bmatrix},$$

will contain a substantial number of zero elements.

[3] Cf. J. M. Clark, "Business Acceleration and the Law of Demand," *Journal of Political Economy*, XXV (March, 1917), 217-235, reprinted in *Readings in Business Cycle Theory*, pp. 235-260; also Ragnar Frisch, "The Interrelation Between Capital Production and Consumer Taking," *Journal of Political Economy*, XXXIX (October, 1931), pp. 646-654, and Gottfried Haberler, *Prosperity and Depression*, as well as works cited by these authors.

[4] P. A. Samuelson, "Interactions Between the Multiplier Analysis and the Principle of Acceleration," *Review of Economic Statistics*, XXI (May, 1939), pp. 75-78, reprinted in *Readings in Business Cycle Theory*, 261-269.

[5] For Samuelson, investment at time t is proportionate to the change in consumption from time $t-1$ to t. This does not leave any time, however, for a lag between the change in consumption and the investment; this lag is allowed for in the above formulation.

With the introduction of these acceleration coefficients, the receipts equation for the i-th sector will read:

(8. 11) $dY_i(t) = dE_1 + \sum_{j=1}^{n} {}_jE'_i dY_j(t-1)$

$$+ \sum_{j=1}^{n} a_{ij}[dY_j(t-1) - dY_j(t-2)].$$

From all n receipts equations, the following matric equation is derived:

(8. 12)

$$dY(t) = dE + M dY(t-1) + A[dY(t-1) - dY(t-2)]$$
$$= dE + [M + A]dY(t-1) - A\, dY(t-2).$$

The equilibrium solution of this system is identical with that of the multiplier:

(8. 13) $\overline{dY} = dE + M\, \overline{dY}$

$$(\overline{dY} = dY(t) = dY(t-1) = dY(t-2)).$$

The dynamic or transient part of the solution is given by the characteristic polynomial of (8. 12):

(8. 14) $|\, I\lambda^2 - (M + A)\lambda + A\,| = 0.$

The properties of this dynamic system are in principle derivable from (8. 14).

The foregoing model is to be taken only as a crude simplification (in spite of its advantages over the aggregative formulation of the acceleration principle), since a simple linear relationship between investment and changes in sales is not in fact characteristic of the real world. At a later date an attempt will be made to remedy this deficiency.

III. CONCLUSION

In our theoretical analysis, the basic properties of the multi-sector multiplier have been derived. These basic properties have to do with (1) the nature of the equilibrium solution, (2) the stability of equilibrium (that is, the ability of the dynamic system to reach the equilibrium of the static system),

(3) the correspondence principle (the principle by which the static system is able to reveal the true dynamic solution), and (4) the nature of the time-path towards, or away from, equilibrium.

With regard to the nature of the equilibrium solution, we found that many equilibrium values are possible. If the restriction is made that all autonomous injections into the economy are in the same direction in every sector, then three cases may be distinguished: (a) if no restriction is put on the sectors' marginal propensities to spend to themselves and to one another, the multiplier may have positive or negative values; (b) if all sectors' marginal propensities to extraspend are nonnegative, the total multiplier for the whole economy must exceed $\frac{1}{2}$; (c) if all sectors' marginal propensities to intraspend as well as extraspend are nonnegative, the total multiplier cannot be less than unity. These equilibrium values of the multiplier are all stable ones; that is to say, the multiplier must converge to those values after an infinite lapse of time.

There also exist unstable equilibrium values. That is, there exist equilibrium solutions which can never be reached, for the slightest disturbances from such equilibria cause the system to move away from them. We found that necessary and sufficient conditions can be stated for the existence of a stable solution. Furthermore, we saw that certain necessary conditions for stability exist. The average of all sectors' marginal propensities to intraspend must be less than unity; and if the marginal propensities to extraspend are all nonnegative, *each* sector's marginal propensity to intraspend must be less than unity.

While the static system provides the equilibrium solutions, it does not always reveal whether these solutions are stable ones towards which the dynamic system will actually converge. Though the static system can sometimes reveal instability (as it does when its determinant is nonpositive), at other times (namely, when the determinant is positive) we cannot always tell, within the static framework, whether or not the equilibrium solutions are possible ones. A purely comparative statical analysis of the multiplier process is therefore an inadequate one.

Dynamic analysis, in addition to providing the conditions of stability, describes the nature of the time-path of the multiplier process. Several propositions were proved with regard to the character of this dynamic system. It was shown that, given three restrictions (in addition to the restrictions of the model [6]), the multiplier process is of necessity monotonic. These three restrictions are (1) that the parameters of the system (the sectors' marginal propensities to spend to themselves and to one another) be nonnegative, (2) that autonomous injections into the economy be of like sign in all sectors, and (3) that these autonomous injections all be monotonic. If any one of these assumptions is relaxed, non-monotonic behavior within the multiplier process is possible.

Oscillations are clearly possible if a sufficient number of parameters are negative. A wave is also possible, since we saw that the multiplier can have negative equilibrium values in these circumstances.

If the second assumption is relaxed, non-monotonic behavior is again possible. A shift in disbursements within the economy may give rise to a wave in a sector's receipts, as Machlup showed; and under certain circumstances, it may give rise to oscillations.

Thirdly, if autonomous injections are not monotonic, oscillations are possible. A single dose of injections may lead to oscillations in individual sector receipts; this is what has been established by Goodwin. Nevertheless there is no *necessity* for the multiplier process to be oscillatory under these circumstances. National income is likely to be less oscillatory the less is the degree of vertical integration of industry. Furthermore, total transactions are likely to be more oscillatory the greater is the disparity among the lags of transactors' disbursements behind their receipts. Finally, if transaction periods are equal, total transactions—given, of course, restrictions (1) and (2) above—cannot be oscillatory unless some transactors have greater than unit, and other have less than unit, marginal

[6] These are the assumptions implied by the model itself, such as the absence of the principle of acceleration. It is not necessary, however, to retain the assumption of rigid prices, since it follows from Section I of this chapter that our conclusions apply just as fully to a linear system in which price changes are introduced.

propensities to spend; similarly, if income periods are equal, total income cannot be oscillatory unless some income recipients have greater than unit, while others have less than unit, marginal propensities to spend.

During the course of our analysis, one fact has emerged repeatedly. The greater is the degree of heterogeneity within the economy, the more abnormal is the behavior of the economy as a whole. If the sectors of the economy are homogeneous among themselves (in the sense that they have equal marginal propensities to spend and that their disbursements follow their receipts after equal time lags), then negative multipliers, and oscillatory and wavelike movement of total receipts, cannot occur. Since there is considerable evidence to the effect that the economy is, in fact, relatively heterogeneous, our aim in this book to set up a model of an economy consisting as much as possible of internally-homogeneous sectors has been justified.

That is not, however, the only accomplishment of this book. Even if the economy were relatively homogeneous, there would still be room for the theory of international and interregional trade, the theory of interindustrial relationships, and the theory of distribution. The theory of the multiplier throws much light on these branches of economic theory.

In spite of the power of multiplier analysis, we must not overlook the limitations inherent in the approach. We have suggested in this chapter how further refinements may be added; it is to be hoped that in the future a more comprehensive theory may be evolved. Empirical application of our model should not be too rashly embarked upon without a thorough realization of the assumptions involved in the model.

BIBLIOGRAPHICAL NOTE

Among the economic writings that were used in this study, the most influential have been the following: Fritz Machlup, *International Trade and the National Income Multiplier*, and " Period Analysis and Multiplier Theory"; Oscar Lange, " The Theory of the Multiplier "; Lloyd A. Metzler, " Underemployment Equilibrium in International Trade"; Paul A. Samuelson, " A Fundamental Multiplier Identity "; R. M. Goodwin, " The Multiplier as Matrix"; and Wassily Leontief, *The Structure of American Economy, 1919-1929*, and " Output, Employment, Consumption, and Investment."

Two important mathematical sources were J. Schur, " über Potenzreihen, die im Innern des Einheitskreis beschränkt sind," and A. Cohn, " über die Anzahl der Wurzeln einer algebraischen Gleichung in einem Kreise."

In addition, certain basic mathematical texts were relied upon. In the field of matrix theory, the following were used: R. A. Frazer, W. J. Duncan and A. R. Collar, *Elementary Matrices and Some Applications to Dynamics and Differential Equations* (New York, 1947); Cyrus Colton MacDuffee, *Vectors and Matrices* (Menasha, Wisconsin, 1943); and A. C. Aitken, *Determinants and Matrices*. On the theory of difference equations, the following writings were consulted: F. R. Moulton, *Differential Equations* (New York, 1930), Chapter XV; Paul A. Samuelson, "Dynamic Process Analysis," *A Survey of Contemporary Economics*, edited by Howard E. Ellis (Philadelphia, 1948); and R. G. D. Allen, " Mathematical Foundations of Economic Theory," *Quarterly Journal of Economics*, LXIII (February, 1949), pp. 111-127.

INDEX

Acceleration principle, 17, 140-142, 144 n.
Aggregates, partial, 51.
Aggregation, 13, 50, 51, 56, 137.
Aggregative economics, 13, 134, 142.
Aggregative general equilibrium, see Equilibrium.
Aggregative multiplier analysis, see Multiplier Analysis.
Aitken, A. C., *Determinants and Matrices*, 112 n.
Artificial barriers, 49.
Automatic responses, 73.
Autonomous changes, 53, 54, 62, 64, 66, 68, 70, 72, 82, 84 n., 85, 87 n., 92, 93, 114, 118, 122, 125, 126, 127, 129, 134, 135, 138, 139, 144. *See also*, Disturbance, Exogenous changes, Injections.
Average marginal propensity to spend, 130, 132.
Average propensity to spend, 30 n.

Balance of payments, 25 n., 29, 36.
Banking system, 26, 29, 31.
Bastable, C. F., *Theory of International Trade*, 15 n., 54 n.
Bill of goods, 16.
Borrowing, 24, 25, 26, 29, 37; net foreign, 63, 69, 71, 72, 74.
Bretherton, R. F., Burchardt, F. A., and Rutherford, R. S. G., *Public Investment and the Trade Cycle*, 14 n., 93 n.
Budget, balanced, 32, 35, 64.
Budget deficit, 25, 64, 77.
Budget surplus, 64.
Budgets, government, 23.
Burchardt, F. A., *see* Bretherton, R. F., Burchardt, F. A., and Rutherford, R. S. G.
Business, 22-35, 41, 46, 47, 48, 50 n., 52, 53, 57, 80, 99, 121, 134, 135, 136.
Business activity, 23.
Business capital and debt, 27, 28, 35, 36.

Business establishments, 23.
Business gains and losses, 38.
Business psychology, 17.
Business taxes, 27, 28, 36.

Cairnes, J. E., *Some Leading Principles of Political Economy*, 15 n., 54 n.
Cambridge school, 44.
Canada, regional differences in, 57 n.
Capital: consumption of, 37, 38; fixed, 141.
Capital equipment, 37, 38, 44.
Capital goods, 30 n., 141. *See also*, Durable goods.
Capital outlay, 36, 37.
Capitalists, 15, 29, 30, 36, 52, 54, 74, 77.
Cash balances, 35.
Cassel, Gustav, 51.
Channels of payment, 33, 34, 54.
Characteristic equation (polynomial), 101, 102, 118, 120, 142.
Chipman, J. S.: "The Generalized Bi-System Multiplier," 9, 10, 61 n., 64 n.
"The Multi-Sector Multiplier," 9; "Professor Goodwin's Matrix Multiplier," 9, 125 n.
Circular flow, 26.
Clark, J. M., 93 n.; "Business Acceleration and the Law of Demand," 141 n.
Classes, 14, 15, 29, 52, 54, 121.
Classical economics, 16, 18, 32, 34, 35.
Clifford, A. H., 11, 112 n., 114.
Closed economy, 14, 79.
Cohn, A., 119, 120; "Über die Anzahl der Wurzeln einer algebraischen Gleichung in einem Kreise," 119 n.
Cohn conditions, 120.
Collecting, 26, 29.
Collecting agencies, 17, 41, 45, 46, 47, 53, 57, 99, 133, 134.
Commodities: manufactured, 27, 28, 50;

147

THE JOHNS HOPKINS UNIVERSITY

STUDIES IN

HISTORICAL AND POLITICAL SCIENCE

◂ ◂ ◂

SIXTY-EIGHTH SERIES (1950)
(Complete in three numbers)

◂ ◂ ◂

A subscription for the regular annual series is $5.00. Single numbers may be purchased at special prices. A complete list of the series is given on pages v-xii.

i

THE WALTER HINES PAGE SCHOOL OF INTERNATIONAL RELATIONS

THE PROTECTION OF NATIONALS: A Study in the Application of International Law. By FREDERICK SHERWOOD DUNN. *238 pages, $2.25*
" I can comment only in superlatives. It is splendid, perfectly splendid! "
—EDWIN D. DICKINSON, *University of Michigan Law School*

THE RUSSO-JAPANESE TREATIES OF 1907-1916 CONCERNING MANCHURIA AND MONGOLIA. By ERNEST B. PRICE. *176 pages, $1.75*
" Invaluable to scholars seeking a clearer understanding of the present conflict of interests between the Soviet Union and Japan." —*The Nation*

A STUDY OF CHINESE BOYCOTTS with Special Reference to Their Economic Effectiveness. By C. F. REMER with the assistance of WILLIAM B. PALMER. *318 pages, $2.75*
This volume " will be of interest not merely to the student of the commerce and politics of the Far East, but also to political scientists generally."
—TYLER DENNETT, *American Political Science Review*

A VIEW OF EUROPE, 1932: An Interpretative Essay on Some Workings of Economic Nationalism. By PAUL VAN ZEELAND. *162 pages, $1.75*
" The book will commend itself to many general readers and not a few specialists."—JOHN DONALDSON.
Annals of the American Academy of Political and Social Science

MANIFEST DESTINY: A Study of Nationalist Expansionism in American History. By ALBERT K. WEINBERG. *572 pages, $4.50*
" If it is true that the world is on the verge of a new epoch in imperialism, initiated by the Japanese invasion of China and the Italian crusade against Ethiopia, then the publication of this book is both timely and embarrassing . . . because it reveals that the United States, now definitely hostile to expansionism on the part of other nations, has justified the taking of territory in the past by arguments even more shoddy than those today advanced by Italy or Japan." . . .
—RAYMOND LESLIE BUELL, *New York Herald Tribune Books*

INTERVENTION, CIVIL WAR, AND COMMUNISM IN RUSSIA. APRIL-DECEMBER 1918: DOCUMENTS AND MATERIALS. By JAMES BUNYAN. *610 pages. $4.50*
" The volume covers the critical months of 1918, when everything seemed to indicate that the Soviet government, established in Moscow, had no chance to survive." —LEONID I. STRAKHOVSKY, *The Journal of Modern History*

THE ORIGINS OF THE FOREIGN POLICY OF WOODROW WILSON. By HARLEY NOTTER. *702 pages, $4.50*
To examine the foreign policy of President Wilson is to examine one of the most decisive factors in the contemporary history of the United States and of the world.

THE UNITED STATES AND SANTO DOMINGO 1798-1873. A Chapter in Caribbean Diplomacy. By CHARLES CALLAN TANSILL. *497 pages, $3.50*
Dr. Tansill has made effective use of the records in the Foreign Offices of France, Germany, and Great Britain, together with materials taken from the manuscripts in the Department of State and other American sources.

THE ORIGIN OF MANCHU RULE IN CHINA: Frontier and Bureaucracy as interacting Forces in the Chinese Empire. By FRANZ MICHAEL. *135 pages, map, $2.00*
Mr. Michael shows just what really happened during the last " barbarian " conquest of China, when the Manchus set up a dynasty that lasted from 1644 to the founding of the Chinese Republic in 1911. And by so doing he shows the vital difference between past invasions and conquests of China and the much more sinister " New Order " of institutionalized helotry which Japan is trying to create in the name of a " Greater East Asia."

THE JOHNS HOPKINS PRESS · BALTIMORE 18

ALBERT SHAW LECTURES ON DIPLOMATIC HISTORY

Under the Auspices of the Walter Hines Page
School of International Relations

Duodecimo, cloth

iii

A REPRINT OF ECONOMIC TRACTS

FOUNDED BY JACOB H. HOLLANDER

Octavo, Paper

The first series and numbers one, three and four of the second were out of print for many years but due to a continued demand for them they have been reprinted by planograph.

First Series

1. Three Letters on "The Price of Gold." By DAVID RICARDO. London, 1809. $1.00.
2. An Inquiry into the Nature and Progress of Rent. By T. R. MALTHUS. London, 1815. $1.00.
3. Essay on the Application of Capital to Land. By EDWARD WEST. London, 1866. $1.00.
4. A Refutation of the Wage-Fund Theory. By FRANCIS D. LONGE. London, 1866. $1.00.

Second Series

1. Discourse of Trade. By NICHOLAS BARBON. London, 1690. $1.00.
2. Several Assertions Proved. By JOHN ASGILL. London, 1696. (out of print).
3. Discourses upon Trade. By DUDLEY NORTH. London, 1691. $1.00.
4. Englands Interest and Improvement. By SAMUEL FORTREY. Cambridge, 1663. (out of print).

Third Series

1. The Querist, containing several queries proposed to the consideration of the public. Parts I, II, III. By GEORGE BERKLEY. Dublin, 1735-37. $1.00.
2. An Essay on the Governing Causes of the Natural Rate of Interest; wherein the sentiments of Sir William Petty and Mr. Locke, on that head, are considered. By JOSEPH MASSIE. London, 1750. 50 cents.
3. Money answers all Things: or an essay to make money sufficiently plentiful amongst all ranks of people, and increase our foreign and domestick trade. By JACOB VANDERLINT. London, 1734. $1.00.
4. An Essay on Ways and Means for Raising Money for the support of the present war, without increasing the public debts. By FRANCIS FAUQUIER. London, 1756. 50 cents.

Fourth Series

1. Letters of John Ramsay McCulloch to David Ricardo, 1818-1823. $1.00.
2. Observations on the Effects of the Corn Laws and of a Rise or Fall in the Price of Corn on the Agriculture and General Wealth of the Country. By T. R. MALTHUS. London, 1814. $1.00.
3. Observations on the circumstances which Influence the Condition of the Labouring Classes of Society. By JOHN BARTON. London, 1817. $1.00.
4. Two Letters on the Measures of Value Contributed to the Traveller (London) in December 1822. By JOHN STUART MILL. $1.00.

Fifth Series

1. Two Tracts by Gregory King:
   (a). Natural and Political Observations and Conclusions upon the State and Condition of England. 1696.
   (b). Of the Naval Trade of England A° 1688 and the National Profit then arising thereby. 1697. MS.
   Edited with an Introduction by GEORGE E. BARNETT. $1.50
2. Natural and Political Observations Mentioned in a following Index and made upon the Bills of Mortality. By JOHN GRAUNT. London, 1676. With an introduction by WALTER F. WILLCOX. $1.25.
3. Two papers on the Degrees of Mortality of Mankind. 1693. By EDMUND HALLEY. Introduction and notes by LOWELL J. REED. $1.25.
4. (a). A Memorial Concerning the Coyn of England. 1695. MS. (b). A Memoriall Concerning Creditt. 1696. MS. Two Manuscripts. By CHARLES DAVENANT, with an Introduction by ABBOTT PAYSON USHER. $1.75.

THE JOHNS HOPKINS PRESS   BALTIMORE 18

THE JOHNS HOPKINS UNIVERSITY STUDIES IN
HISTORICAL AND POLITICAL SCIENCE

* Not sold separately.

FIRST SERIES.—1883.

(Complete volume out of print.)

I. An Introduction to American Institutional History. By E. A. FREEMAN. 25 cents.
*II. The Germanic Origin of New England Towns. By H. B. ADAMS.
III. Local Government in Illinois. By ALBERT SHAW.—Local Government in Pennsylvania. By E. R. L. GOULD. 30 cents.
IV. Saxon Tithingmen in America. By H. B. ADAMS. 50 cents.
V. Local Government in Michigan and the Northwest. By E. W. BEMIS. 25 cents.
VI. Parish Institutions of Maryland. By EDWARD INGLE. 40 cents.
VII. Old Maryland Manors. By JOHN HEMSLEY JOHNSON. (O. P.)
VIII. Norman Constables in America. By H. B. ADAMS. 50 cents.
IX–X. Village Communities of Cape Ann and Salem. By H. B. ADAMS. 50 cents.
XI. The Genesis of a New England State. By A. JOHNSTON. 30 cents.
*XII. Local Government and Schools in South Carolina. By B. J. RAMAGE.

SECOND SERIES.—1884.

(Complete volume out of print.)

*I–II. Methods of Historical Study. By H. B. ADAMS.
III. The Past and Present of Political Economy. By R. T. ELY. 35 cents.
IV. Samuel Adams, the Man of the Town Meeting. By JAMES K. HOSMER. 35 cents.
V–VI. Taxation in the United States. By HENRY CARTER ADAMS. 50 cents.
VII. Institutional Beginnings in a Western State. By JESSE MACY. 25 cents.
VIII–IX. Indian Money in New England, etc. By WILLIAM B. WEEDEN. 50 cents.
X. Town and County Government in the Colonies. By E. CHANNING. (O. P.)
*XI. Rudimentary Society among Boys. By J. HEMSLEY JOHNSON.
XII. Land Laws of Mining Districts. By C. H. SHINN. 50 cents.

THIRD SERIES.—1885.—$4.00.

I. Maryland's Influence upon Land Cessions to the U. S. By H. B. ADAMS. 75 cents.
*II–III. Virginia Local Institutions. By E. INGLE.
IV. Recent American Socialism. By RICHARD T. ELY. 50 cents.
V–VI–VII. Maryland Local Institutions. By LEWIS W. WILHELM. $1.00.
VIII. Influence of the Proprietors in Founding New Jersey. By A. SCOTT. 25 cents.
IX–X. American Constitutions. By HORACE DAVIS. (O. P.)
*XI–XII. The City of Washington. By J. A. PORTER.

FOURTH SERIES.—1886.—$4.00.

I. Dutch Village Communities on the Hudson River. By I. ELTING. (O. P.)
*II–III. Town Government in Rhode Island. By W. E. FOSTER.—The Narragansett Planters. By EDWARD CHANNING.
IV. Pennsylvania Boroughs. By WILLIAM P. HOLCOMB. 50 cents.
*V. Introduction to Constitutional History of the States. By J. F. JAMESON.
VI. The Puritan Colony at Annapolis, Maryland. By D. R. RANDALL. 50 cents.
*VII–VIII–IX. The Land Question in the United States. By S. SATO.
X. Town and City Government of New Haven. By C. H. LEVERMORE. 50 cents.
*XI–XII. Land System of the New England Colonies. By M. EGLESTON.

FIFTH SERIES.—1887.—$4.00.

I–II. City Government of Philadelphia. By E. P. ALLINSON and B. PENROSE. (O. P.)
III. City Government of Boston. By JAMES M. BUGBEE. (O. P.)
*IV. City Government of St. Louis. By MARSHALL S. SNOW.
V–VI. Local Government in Canada. By JOHN GEORGE BOURINOT. 50 cents.

VII. Effect of the War of 1812 upon American Union. By N. M. BUTLER. (O. P.)
VIII. Notes on the Literature of Charities. By HERBERT B. ADAMS. 25 cents.
IX. Predictions of Hamilton and De Tocqueville. By JAMES BRYCE. (O. P.)
X. The Study of History in England and Scotland. By P. FREDERICQ. 25 cents.
XI. Seminary Libraries and University Extension. By H. B. ADAMS. 25 cents.
*XII. European Schools of History and Politics. By A. D. WHITE.

SIXTH SERIES.—1888.

The History of co-operation in the United States. (O. P.)

SEVENTH SERIES.—1889.
(Complete volume out of print.)

I. Arnold Toynbee. By F. C. MONTAGUE. 50 cents.
II-III. Municipal Government in San Francisco. By BERNARD MOSES. 50 cents.
IV. Municipal History of New Orleans. By WM. W. HOWE. 25 cents.
V-VI. English Culture in Virginia. By WILLIAM P. TRENT. (O. P.)
VII-VIII-IX. The River Towns of Connecticut. By CHARLES M. ANDREWS. $1.00.
X-XI-XII. Federal Government in Canada. By JOHN G. BOURINOT. (O. P.)

EIGHTH SERIES.—1889.
(Complete volume out of print.)

I-II. The Beginnings of American Nationality. By A. W. SMALL. $1.00.
III. Local Government in Wisconsin. By D. E. SPENCER. 25 cents.
IV. Spanish Colonization in the Southwest. By F. W. BLACKMAR. (O. P.)
V-VI. The Study of History in Germany and France. By P. FREDERICQ. $1.00.
VII-IX. Progress of the Colored People of Maryland. By J. R. BRACKETT. $1.00.
X. The Study of History in Belgium and Holland. By P. FREDERICQ. (O. P.)
XI-XII. Seminary Notes on Historical Literature. By H. B. ADAMS and others. 50 cents

NINTH SERIES.—1891.
(Volume sold only with complete set.)

*I-II. Government of the United States. By W. W. WILLOUGHBY and W. F. WILLOUGHBY.
III-IV. University Education in Maryland. By B. C. STEINER.—The Johns Hopkins University (1876-1891). By D. C. GILMAN. 50 cents.
*V-VI. Municipal Unity in the Lombard Communes. By W. K. WILLIAMS.
VII-VIII. Public Lands of the Roman Republic. By A. STEPHENSON. 75 cents.
*IX. Constitutional Development of Japan. By T. IYENAGA.
*X. A History of Liberia. By J. H. T. MCPHERSON.
XI-XII. The Indian Trade in Wisconsin. By F. J. TURNER. 50 cents.

TENTH SERIES.—1892.—$4.00.

*I. The Bishop Hill Colony. By MICHAEL A. MIKKELSEN.
II-III. Church and State in New England. By PAUL E. LAUER. 50 cents.
IV. Church and State in Maryland. By GEORGE PETRIE. 50 cents.
V-VI. Religious Development of North Carolina. By S. B. WEEKS. 50 cents.
*VII. Maryland's Attitude in the Struggle for Canada. By J. W. BLACK.
VIII-IX. The Quakers in Pennsylvania. By A. C. APPLEGARTH. 75 cents.
X-XI. Columbus and His Discovery of America. By H. B. ADAMS and H. WOOD. 50 cents.
XII. Causes of the American Revolution. By J. A. WOODBURN. (O. P.)

ELEVENTH SERIES.—1893.—$4.00.

I. The Social Condition of Labor. By E. R. L. GOULD. 50 cents.
II. The World's Representative Assemblies of To-day. By E. K. ALDEN. 50 cents.
III-IV. The Negro in the District of Columbia. By EDWARD INGLE. $1.00.
V-VI. Church and State in North Carolina. By STEPHEN B. WEEKS. (O. P.)
VII-VIII. The Condition of the Western Farmer, etc. By A. F. BENTLEY. $1.00.
IX-X. History of Slavery in Connecticut. By BERNARD C. STEINER. 75 cents.
XI-XII. Local Government in the South. By E. W. BEMIS and others. $1.00.

TWELFTH SERIES.—1894.—$4.00.

I-II. The Cincinnati Southern Railway. By J. H. HOLLANDER. $1.00.
III. Constitutional Beginnings of North Carolina. By J. S. BASSETT. 50 cents.
IV. Struggle of Dissenters for Toleration in Virginia. By H. R. MCILWAINE. 50 cents.
*V-VI-VII. The Carolina Pirates and Colonial Commerce. By S. C. HUGHSON.
VIII-IX. Representation and Suffrage in Massachusetts. By G. H. HAYNES. 50 cents.
X. English Institutions and the American Indian. By J. A. JAMES. 25 cents.
XI-XII. International Beginnings of the Congo Free State. By J. S. REEVES. 50 cents.

vi

viii

x

FIFTIETH SERIES.—1932.—$5.75.

I. Hours of Labor. By LAZARE TEPER. $1.00.
II. Some Presidential Interpretations of the Presidency. By NORMAN J. SMALL. $1.75.
III. The Governor of Maryland. By CHARLES JAMES ROHR. $1.50; cloth, $2.00.
IV. The Yellow Dog Contract. By JOEL I. SEIDMAN. $1.00.

FIFTY-FIRST SERIES.—1933.—$5.75.

I. Studies on Scipio Africanus. By RICHARD M. HAYWOOD. $1.00.
II. The Right of Search and the Slave Trade in Anglo-American Relations, 1814-1862. By HUGH G. SOULSBY. $1.75.
III. American Policy of Recognition Towards Mexico. By STUART A. MacCORKLE. $1.00.
IV. Mathew Carey: A Study in American Economic Development. By KENNETH W. ROWE. $1.25.
V. Hezekiah Niles as an Economist. By RICHARD GABRIEL STONE. $1.25; cloth, $1.75.

FIFTY-SECOND SERIES.—1934.—$5.75.

I. Italy's Relations with England, 1896-1905. By JAMES LINUS GLANVILLE. $1.50.
II. The Capital Issues Committee and War Finance Corporation. By WOODBURY WILLOUGHBY. $1.25.
III. Maryland Business Corporations, 1783-1852. By JOSEPH G. BLANDI. $1.25.
IV. The American Doctrine of State Succession. By HERBERT A. WILKINSON. $1.25.

FIFTY-THIRD SERIES.—1935.—$5.75.

I. The Juristic Status of Egypt and the Sudan. By VERNON A. O'ROURKE. $1.50.
II. Workmen's Compensation in Maryland. By EVELYN ELLEN SINGLETON. $1.25.
III. Mutual Savings Banks in Baltimore. By ROBERT W. THON, JR. $1.25.
IV. Contribution of the Ideologues to French Revolutionary Thought. By C. H. VAN DUZER. $1.50.

FIFTY-FOURTH SERIES.—1936.—$5.75.

I. The Movement for the Acquisition of All Mexico, 1846-1848. By J. D. P. FULLER. $1.50.
II. The Gas Light Company of Baltimore: A Study of Natural Monopoly. By G. T. BROWN. $1.00.
III. The Journeymen Barbers' International Union of America. By W. S. HALL. $1.25.
IV. The Supreme Court and Political Questions. By C. G. POST. $1.25; cloth, $1.75.

FIFTY-FIFTH SERIES.—1937.—$5.75.

I. Germany and Morocco Before 1905. By FRANCIS T. WILLIAMSON. $2.00.
II. History and Development of the Fourth Amendment of the United States Constitution. By NELSON B. LASSON. $1.50.
III. The Influence of Border Troubles on Relations Between the United States and Mexico, 1876-1910. By ROBERT GREGG. $2.00.
IV. The Floating Debt of the Federal Government, 1919-1936. By E. R. VAN SANT. $1.00.

FIFTY-SIXTH SERIES.—1938.—$5.75.

I. Commercial Banking and the Stock Market before 1863. By J. E. HEDGES. $1.50.
II. Industry and Commerce of the City of Rome. 50 B. C.-200 A. D. By HELEN J. LOANE. $1.50.
III. The Investment Value of Goodwill. By L. N. BLOOMBERG. 75 cents.
IV. Historical Scholarship in the United States, 1876-1901: As Revealed in the Correspondence of Herbert B. Adams. Edited by W. S. HOLT. $2.50; cloth, $3.00.

FIFTY-SEVENTH SERIES.—1939.—$5.75.

I. A History of Criminal Syndicalism Legislation in the United States. By E. F. DOWELL. $1.50.
II. The Wholesale Marketing of Fruits and Vegetables in Baltimore. By R. G. DEUPREE. $1.25.
III. The History of the Woman's Peace Party. By M. L. DEGEN. $2.50; cloth, $2.75.

FIFTY-EIGHTH SERIES.—1940.—$5.75

I. Malaria and Colonization in the Carolina Low Country, 1526-1696. By ST. JULIEN RAVENEL CHILDS. $2.50.
II. Municipal Indebtedness: A Study of the Debt-to-Property Ratio. By LEROY A. SHATTUCK, JR. $1.25.
III. The Security Affiliates of National Banks. By WILLIAM NELSON PEACH. $1.50.

xi

THE JOHNS HOPKINS PRESS · BALTIMORE 18

EXTRA VOLUMES OF STUDIES IN HISTORICAL AND POLITICAL SCIENCE

* Out of print

THE JOHNS HOPKINS PRESS · BALTIMORE 18

EXTRA VOLUMES OF STUDIES IN HISTORICAL AND POLITICAL SCIENCE

NEW SERIES
* Out of print

NOTES SUPPLEMENTARY TO THE STUDIES IN HISTORY AND POLITICS

THE JOHNS HOPKINS PRESS · BALTIMORE 18